METROPOLITAN AMERICA

METROPOLITAN AMERICA

Advisory Editor
Richard C. Wade

Research Associate
Eugene P. Moehring

The Country Town

A Study of Rural Evolution

WILBERT L. ANDERSON

ARNO PRESS

A New York Times Company

New York / 1974

Reprint Edition 1974 by Arno Press Inc.

METROPOLITAN AMERICA
ISBN for complete set: 0-405-05380-0
See last pages of this volume for titles.

Manufactured in the United States of America

———————◆———————

Library of Congress Cataloging in Publication Data

Anderson, Wilbert Lee, 1857-1915.
    The country town.

    (Metropolitan America)
    Reprint of the 1906 ed. published by Baker & Taylor,
New York.
    1. Sociology, Rural. 2. Social problems.
I. Title. II. Series.
HT431.A6 1974   301.35   73-11914
ISBN 0-405-05382-7

The Country Town

The Country Town

A Study of Rural Evolution

By
WILBERT L. ANDERSON

With an Introduction by
JOSIAH STRONG

NEW YORK
THE BAKER & TAYLOR CO.
33–37 EAST SEVENTEENTH STREET, UNION SQ., NORTH

To my Father and my Mother
I offer this book
in appreciation of their witness
to whatever is best
in rural life.

Preface

SCIENCE has the difficult task of correcting the illusions of the senses. The heavens and the atoms alike deceive the observer, and in history, also, things are not what they seem. The social fact thrusting itself upon impression has another character when placed under the laws of progress. One group of observations has peculiar need of interpretation—radical changes in the rural population meet the eye everywhere, of which crass misjudgment passes from lip to lip and from page to page of print. There are hints of an alarming natural selection in depleted communities, but we search in vain for the chapter of biology that tells the tale of changing types of men in country towns. It is time to attempt a careful survey of this whole region, into which adventurers have pressed rashly, and from which explorers have brought disheartening reports.

If to tell the truth is better than to be an optimist, one may count himself fortunate who can be both truthful and optimistic. This book endeavors to set forth rural changes in their historical, scientific, and social aspects. Incidentally a wide consensus of opinion in disparagement of rural communities is chal-

3

lenged, and the pessimist who haunts the country towns that he regards gloomily is confronted. The reader must judge the argument, which it has seemed worth while to make as thorough as possible at the critical points because the region it traverses affords many an ambush for the advocates of despair. It is hoped that a cheerful view of conditions and tendencies will be easier for those who follow this discussion, and yet the first responsibility is to the truth, which warrants nothing less urgent than a call to brave and patient work throughout the zone of peril. Even scientific diagnosis avails nothing unless remedies are applied, and certainly to refute the pessimist when the hour demands the rescue of a civilization would be no better than fiddling while Rome burned. If this book had the gift of prophecy and knew all mysteries and all knowledge, if it had all faith so as to remove mountains, and did not prompt the deeds of love, it would be nothing. The country town needs sympathy and calls for help.

My indebtedness to other writers is acknowledged wherever I have drawn directly from them. Among those who have assisted me with suggestion and encouragement I mention gratefully Mr. Edward T. Hartman, Secretary of the Massachusetts Civic League; Mr. Frederick H. Fowler, Clerk of the Massachusetts Board of Agriculture; the Rev. Charles Allen Dinsmore, D. D., with whom almost every point of view has been discussed; and my sister, Miss Mary P. Anderson, whose criticisms have corrected and enriched the entire book, but especially the chapter treating of nature study. The United States Census Office and the United States Department of Agriculture generously supplied me with indispensable publications.

Finally, I am under the greatest obligation to the Rev. Josiah Strong, D.D., whose inspiring and thorough social studies opened to me this field of investigation.

WILBERT L. ANDERSON.

Exeter, New Hampshire.

CONTENTS

BOOK I

THE CHANGED WORLD

BOOK II

THE QUESTION OF CHARACTER

BOOK III

THE INCIDENCE OF SELECTION

BOOK IV

THE DIRECT ACTION OF ENVIRONMENT

BOOK V

SOCIAL RECONSTRUCTION

Introduction

THIS is a much needed and valuable book. The author has faith in the future of the country town, and is able to render a reason for the faith that is in him. His confidence is based on the results of a close and scientific scrutiny of the complex influences which are at work upon the population of country communities.

Much has been said, and truly, of the removal of the upper stratum of country society to the city. When population is seriously depleted, roads deteriorate, communication becomes more difficult, the church and the school suffer, and it is those who place the highest valuation on religious and educational advantages for their children who seek those advantages in the city. Thus it is the cream that is skimmed off. If this were the whole truth, it would mean the inevitable degeneracy of the rural population. But while the author recognizes the loss of the old country aristocracy, he calls attention to the fact that the industrial revolution has also driven the lowest stratum of society from country to city,—a stratum which was not created, though it may have been augmented, by the influences of existing conditions, but is composed of the unfit who as descendants of the unfit have gravitated to the bottom, generation after generation.

Families run out both at the top and at the bottom of the social scale. It is the great middle class which from the point of view of the evolutionist constitutes the hope of society; and it is precisely this class which remains in the country.

The author, therefore, concludes, and very justly, "that there is no scientific reason for the popular notion that the rural population is under a fatality of evil. Its future depends almost wholly upon the power of environment,—upon education, upon commerce, upon evangelization, upon participation in the great movements of the age."

The introduction of the rural mail delivery, the extension of the telephone system into the country, and easy communication with the city by means of the electric road, will all improve the country environment. It must not be inferred, however, that these agencies will materially affect the drift towards the city; that is determined almost wholly by economic causes. Some thousands of men work under ground, not because they prefer the darkness and danger, the smut and wet of a coal mine, to God's blue sky and the green earth, but because there is a demand for coal. And the number of miners is determined by the magnitude of that demand, not by the measure of comfort or discomfort in mining. Pleasant or unpleasant conditions of work determine the *class* of people, but not the *number* of people, who will engage in it.

The improvement of the country environment, therefore, will have the double effect of elevating the country population and of attracting a better class to agriculture.

The object of this volume, accordingly, is to excite interest in the problem of the necessary social reconstruction, the improved environment, of the country town.

The author gives us the inspiration of a rational hope that this problem can be and will be solved by " generous deeds, tireless diligence, and stedfast patience."

JOSIAH STRONG.

BOOK I

THE CHANGED WORLD

"If we would study with profit the history of our ancestors, we must be constantly on our guard against that delusion which the well-known names of families, places, and offices naturally produce, and must never forget that the country of which we read was a very different country from that in which we live."

　　　　—*Macaulay, " History of England," Vol. I, Chap. III.*

" Now by far the most obvious and constant characteristic common to a vast number of social changes is that they are changes from a worse to a better state of things,—that they constitute phases of Progress. It is not asserted that human history has in all times and places been the history of progress: it is not denied that at various times and in many places it has been the history of retrogression: but attention is called to the fact—made trite by long familiarity, yet none the less habitually misconceived—that progress has been on the whole the most constant and prominent feature of a considerable and important portion of mankind."

　　　　—*John Fiske, " Cosmic Philosophy," Vol. II, p. 192.*

CHAPTER I

THE NEW INDUSTRIAL ORDER

THE present stands in sharp contrast with the recent past in country towns. The memory of living men retains a vivid image of much to which visible conditions offer no parallel, and tradition further glorifies "the good old times." The middle of the nineteenth century may be selected as the most eligible point from which to contemplate the contrasted civilizations. If much that has come to pass could not have been foreseen then, the new form of society was clearly discernible, and the old order was not far out of sight. Happily the most competent man of his time for such a task took advantage of the centennial of a Connecticut county in 1851 to portray the life of the fathers as it lingered radiantly in memory, being himself deeply sensible that a new age had dawned. The hour was opportune for speech immortalizing a unique social order; it was the earliest moment permitting the enchanter's transformation, and a later time would have dulled the personal witness. From that crest of the nineteenth century the orator beheld the life of the fathers in the distance that obscures defect in idealizing lights, and his prophetic eye, penetrating the waiting years, saw that nothing would ever be again as in the old times.

Never was Horace Bushnell happier in the choice of terms than when he called that vanished epoch " The Age of Homespun."[1] We see men clad in the wool clipped from their own flocks, women wearing the product of their looms ; and at once we know their industrial order, their manner of life, and their virtues. The thread from the home spindle is the clew to every passage in their civilization. With great zest the orator shows how in an age of homespun there are flocks of sheep in the pastures, flax growing in the fields, spinning-wheels buzzing and looms thwacking in the house ; how food as well as clothing is produced on the farm, with the slight exception that the lads must go on horseback to mill ; how trade is scant and money little used ; how families thrive in sturdy independence of the world but united in the closest domestic coöperation and affection ; how character grows frugal, austere, honest ; how common ideals and an approximate equality favor friendly intercourse ; how thrift is linked to intelligence and establishes the school ; how these sturdy traits culminate in the earnest discharge of duty towards the Infinite Source of all good in solemn and heart-searching worship. There is such magic in this phrase that as an entire social order develops before the eye, one can scarcely tell whether he is the victim of enchantment or is beholding soberly the course of actual history.

Born in 1802, Dr. Bushnell was able to draw from his own memory the " Arcadian pictures " of his rural idyll. As late as 1810, the country people of the

[1] Horace Bushnell, " Work and Play," p. 374.

United States were generally clad in homespun.   This was no longer the case in 1851, but the memory of the orator easily reached backwards to the reality over which played the transfiguring light of his eloquence. He spoke to those who "recalled the fact that our Litchfield County people down to a period comparatively recent have been a people clothed in homespun fabrics—not wholly or in all cases, but so generally that the exceptions may be fairly disregarded."   Fortunately we are not dependent for the facts upon the uncertain recollection of a later time.   In 1810, Albert Gallatin, Secretary of the Treasury, presented to Congress his "Report on American Manufactures," in which the results of an investigation prosecuted in every state and in more than sixty different places were summarized.   In that report he expresses the opinion "that about two thirds of the clothing, including hosiery, and of the house and table linen worn and used by the inhabitants of the United States who do not reside in cities is the product of family manufactures."[1]   The census of 1810 attempted to gather full statistics of manufactures, and the data collected were submitted to Tench Coxe for arrangement and comment.   His report, published in 1814, thrills with the enthusiasm of a prophet who saw the impending changes in the mode of production, and it is at the same time the best witness concerning the earlier order.[2]   One has but to turn the pages and observe the

[1] "American State Papers," Vol. 10, Finance 2, p. 427.
[2] A Statement of the Arts and Manufactures of the United States of America for the year 1810.

yards of cloth produced in families and in establishments in the several states to see the justice of the
characterization of the time as an age of homespun.
In Pennsylvania, for example, for which the statistics
are the most carefully gathered, 611,481 yards of cotton and 997,346 yards of woollen cloth were produced
in families and only 65,326 yards of cotton and 30,666
yards of woollen cloth were produced in establishments.
The proportion is similar in all the states.

It should be remembered, also, that homespun had
its greatest honor just before it was superseded. The
embargo of 1807 cut off the importation of textiles.
Indeed Gallatin's investigation was prompted by the
sudden development of manufactures when the customary sources of supply were no longer available, and
his report speaks of " an extraordinary increase during
the last two years." A patriotic people caught the vision of complete industrial independence; enthusiasm
ran so high that an effort was made to pledge the members of Congress to wear American goods when engaged in the public service. These were not necessarily of the homespun sort, for the factory was beginning to place a scant product in the market. The
embargo and the war that followed gave such protection to manufactures that by 1820 the modern form of
production was well established, and the change in the
dress of the people was noticeable. The stimulus fell
first, however, upon household manufactures, especially
in the South, where the people had depended upon ex-
changing agricultural products for English goods.
Naturally Jefferson was an enthusiast for the incidental

results of the embargo upon which he had stoutly insisted.[1]

It was, however, the personal experience of the profitableness of the new industries that appealed most powerfully to the thrifty mind of this very practical philosopher and statesman; the production of two thousand yards of cotton, linen, and woollen cloth on his own spinning-jennies and looms—a new feature on his estate—provoked an elation which is evident in several of his letters. One of the most notable of these is that to John Adams, written in 1812. It begins with thanks for specimens of homespun, which suggest a glowing paragraph. " Here we do little in a fine way," he says, " but in coarse and middling goods a great deal. Every family in the country is a manufactory within itself, and is very generally able to make within itself all the stouter and middling stuffs for its own clothing and household use. . . . For fine stuff we shall depend on your northern manufactories. Of these, that is to say of company establishments, we have none. We use little machinery. The spinning-jenny and loom with the flying-shuttle can be managed in a family, but nothing more complicated. The economy and thriftiness resulting from our household manufactures are such that they will never again be laid aside ; and nothing more salutary for us has ever happened than the British obstructions to our demands for their manufactures." What could be more naïve than this pledge of perpetual fidelity to the household

[1] " The Writings of Thomas Jefferson," Vol. VI, p. 36. See also pp. 69, 94.

crafts on a southern plantation at the very moment when they were about to disappear forever ? If they awoke such ardor in a social order that had spurned them, what must have been the revived interest within the proper homespun area ?

Earlier witnesses confirm the view that the use of homespun was extraordinary in Gallatin's time. A report of the governor of Massachusetts to the Board of Trade about 1731 asserted that the country people then made but one-third of their own woollen clothing. Throughout the eighteenth century there were revivals of interest in these domestic manufactures. Thus in 1749, three hundred " young female spinsters " under the direction of the Boston Society for Promoting Industry and Frugality, spun on the common, where weavers also were engaged at their looms. A building seems to have been erected for the purposes of this " spinning craze," which enlisted social enthusiasm and was fostered by anniversary sermons.[1] The Stamp Act provoked this spirit into yet more striking displays; political feeling united with industrial necessity, so that the clothing that otherwise might have been deemed uncouth was marked with social and patriotic distinction. The century probably showed an increase in the production and use of homespun from its beginning to its close.

This development suggests that at an earlier stage homespun was little used. The first period differs radically from subsequent times. The people were

[1] William B. Weeden, " Economic and Social History of New England," Vol. II, pp. 495, 679, 680.

too busy with lumbering and ship-building and fishing, with subduing the land and building homes, to find it possible or profitable to establish household industries. At that time, too, wool and flax were lacking, and it may be questioned whether appliances for spinning and weaving and skill in those crafts were available for the pioneers. When the frontier had been pushed much farther back, we find the settlers at the edge of the wilderness dependent upon the older communities for these supplies. The household crafts do not thrive until the first heavy labors are past, homes securely established, and the means gathered for industrial independence. The peculiarity of the seventeenth century in New England was the nearness of the frontier to the sea,—trade being as important as in the development of civilization along the deeply indented shores of Greece. In these conditions, a division of labor was fostered under which imports from England were distributed to the very edge of the wilderness.

The conditions were not favorable for the homespun civilization until the line of the frontier was separated some scores of miles from the advanced line of commerce. Perhaps no spot was situated more typically in this regard than that upon which Dr. Bushnell pronounced the eulogy of the age of homespun. It was as far from the frontier and as remote from navigable water as any section of New England. Parts of New York and Pennsylvania supplied similar conditions, but the southern colonies, notably Virginia with its long stretches of tide-water, had no space for isolated communities. The settlement of the West fell within another era when changes in transportation caused the line of commerce to follow the frontier closely. The typical homespun civilization, therefore, is found only where settlements had reached maturity before the time of canals and railroads. Where the conditions deflected communities from the pure homespun type, an approximation to this social order was found. Only by observing the peculiar features of this society, can we understand the rural community of a former time or measure the extent of changes that have taken place within it.

By the second decade of the nineteenth century new instruments of textile manufacture were available. The marvellous series of inventions beginning with the fly-shuttle about 1750 included the carding machine, the spinning frame and spinning-mule, and the power loom, when in 1793 Eli Whitney added the cotton-gin. This intricate and ingenious machinery has been subject to constant improvement, so that to this day the discarding of machines before they are worn out is a heavy item of expenditure. The power loom waited for other inventions to make its use profitable,—carding, spinning, and weaving, by machinery, not taking place in one establishment until 1813; but in 1790 a cotton mill and in 1794 a woollen mill were in successful operation in the United States. Meanwhile the steam-engine had been introduced into the factory. When about 1810 the demand for American production became urgent, the pressure fell upon the new method, to the lasting relief of overburdened households. The effect of the new inventions upon

the form of society was discerned almost from the
first. Tench Coxe prefaced his statistical tables with
an introduction that reads like an apocalypse. " The
wonderful machines," he says, " working as if they
were animated beings, endowed with all the talents of
their inventors, laboring with organs that never tire,
and subject to no expense of food, or bed, or raiment,
or dwelling, may be justly considered as equivalent to
an immense body of manufacturing recruits, suddenly
enlisted in the service of the country." [1]

The factory system, on the scale of a new social
order, would not have been practicable without more
efficient modes of transportation than were at hand in
the age of homespun. The first decade of the last
century brought internal improvements to public attention, but at the time little was accomplished except
to plan an elaborate system of canals. The steam-
boat did not appear until 1807, and the railway with
steam traction dates from about 1830. Before 1810
commerce and travel were limited to the natural water-
ways and slow and costly movement along the poor
roads. There was a great enthusiasm in turnpiking at
the beginning of the last century; at the close of its
first decade one hundred and eighty turnpike corporations had been chartered in New England, and almost
as many more had been launched in New York.[2] This
late interest in good roads, coming just as the canal
and the railway were to provide new modes of trans-

[1] " Arts and Manufactures in the United States," p. xxv.
[2] John Bach McMaster, " A History of the People of the United
States," Vol. III, p. 463.

portation, marks the growing discontent with the pitiful isolation of the age of homespun. Merchandise
and produce that could not stand a freight charge of
fifteen dollars per ton could not be carried overland to
a consumer one hundred and fifty miles from the point
of production; as roads were, a distance of fifty miles
from market often made industrial independence expedient.[1]   Where the produce of the farms could not be
sold, where wood and lumber were not marketable, the
people had no resource but to raise their own wool
and flax, and spin and weave and make their own
clothing.   Other crafts felt these influences, although
the working of wood and metals and leather fell to
skilled artisans in the villages rather than to the household.   The local store had a small traffic in articles
that could not be produced, and in luxuries.   Salt fish
was widely distributed; rum went everywhere; salt
was a universal necessity; tools and utensils and furniture were imported; a few articles of dress carried
the style of the city to the hamlet.   So insignificant
was the traffic uniting the country town to the great
world.[2]

[1] " Taking the country through, it may be said that to transport
goods, wares, or merchandise cost ten dollars per ton per hundred
miles.   Articles that could not stand these rates were shut from market,
and among these were grain and flour, which could not bear transportation more than one hundred and fifty miles."   McMaster, Op. Cit.,
p. 464.   Cf. Macaulay, " History of England, Vol. I, Chap. III.

[2] Economic independence is illustrated in an old inventory which
mentions nine hundred and one nails as part of the estate,—the product,
doubtless, of patient hammering by the fireside.   Charles H. Bell,
" History of Exeter, N. H.," p. 329.

The age of homespun was further characterized by the use of hand tools for nearly all the work of the farm. The first half of the nineteenth century bears the same relation to the invention of agricultural implements as the last half of the eighteenth century to the invention of textile machinery. In 1800 the hoe, the scythe, the sickle or the cradle, and the flail were as little displaced as the primitive cards, the spinning-wheel, the warping bars, and the hand loom fifty years earlier. The first decade of the century brought important improvements in the plow; the mowing-machine and the reaper came in the thirties; the horse-rake and the threshing-machine operated by horse power were little used until after 1840. The middle of the century was reached before the more important inventions had overcome popular prejudice. The still more recent rotary milk separator has removed the making of butter from the household in a manner analogous to the transfer of the textile crafts to the factory. A statement in a special report in the census of 1880 purports to gather up the opinions of competent observers concerning the efficiency of improved agricultural implements, and this estimate has been quoted by so many writers of authority that it may be accepted as a true account of conditions a quarter of a century ago: " It is, in fact, estimated by careful men, thoroughly conversant with the changes that have taken place, that in the improvement made in agricultural tools, the average farmer can, with sufficient horse power, do with three men the work of fifteen men forty years ago, and do it

better." [1] This declaration is sufficiently impressive
without revising it to cover the changes of the last
decade.

Rural evolution, as manifest in our time, consists
essentially in the adjustment to new conditions as the
transition from the age of homespun to the age of
machinery is made. The fact of critical importance,
through its relation to the social structure and to the
evolutionary forces, is the altered density of the rural
population. In subsequent chapters an attempt will
be made to measure the ebb and flow of population
in country towns ; here it is desirable to set this
general movement, which is plain to every observer,
in its relation to the change in the mechanical equipment of industry. In all towns not favored by the
new development of manufacturing and trade, there
are fewer people than once dwelt in them. The loss
is accounted for, in part, by the removal of manufactures from families to establishments,—to use the
terms employed by Tench Coxe. The village crafts
have suffered a similar fate, and the displacement of
skilled men is a most serious injury. The reduction
of the force employed on the farms is considerable,
although it cannot be so great as many discussions of
the subject suggest. It is common to pass from the
statement of the efficiency of labor equipped with
modern agricultural implements to the loss of rural
population, as if eleven of fifteen men had become
superfluous. A diminution of workers in the ratio of

[1] Tenth Census, U. S., Vol. II, " Report on the Manufactures of
Interchangeable Mechanism," p. 76.

the increased efficiency of implements, if it were possible, would shatter society beyond recovery. It is evident that nothing so ominous has occurred, for statistics supply the proof that only one or two of that supposed band of eleven ever existed on the farms. There are many reasons why the shrinkage of the farm population is less than the efficiency of machinery suggests. The number of men on the farm is determined largely by the demand for labor in operations that do not permit the use of machinery, as appears most decisively in dairying. The tendency, also, is to enlarge the amount of work done rather than to cut down the number of laborers. Not only are farms cultivated more thoroughly, but a vast production for the market has been added to the volume of agricultural industry. In fact the average farmer has changed and enlarged his business, so that he employs a great part of the labor force formerly required. The hours of work have been shortened notably; the seasons of plowing and seeding, of haymaking and harvesting, have been contracted; the strain of toil has been reduced; the standard of living has been raised,—all this the machine has made possible. Nevertheless when all corrections of current exaggeration have been made, it will be found that the use of improved agricultural implements has seriously diminished the rural population.

The first effect of farm machinery is the hastening of the departure of the farmer's boy from the home. In the age of homespun, sons remained with their fathers until marriage more frequently than in our day. This was partly because no other course was possible, and partly, also, because they were needed for the work now performed by the machine. The substitution of the machine for the lad delaying at home is a great economic and social benefit in spite of the loss through the early sundering of the family. Certainly the boy thrust out of his early home and the greater world which has received him cordially have suffered no injury, for this country boy has had a great career. His success has been due largely to the practical education of the farm; the many arts and crafts of the farm and the farmhouse, though fewer than formerly, still afford excellent manual training, —a more and more evident necessity in a working world. "The best schoolhouse in the world," says a Yale professor, "is an eastern farm . . . where a variety of crops are produced and a variety of work goes on."[1] In city schools it has been found necessary to provide an education of hand and eye and the contriving faculties, which is the birthright of country children. The chapter of history relating the achievements in the city of the young people from the farms is only suggested here, where the point of concern is that the efficient and promising boy was needed at home only at special seasons, as the times for planting, haying, and harvesting. A true economy

[1] William H. Brewer, "The Brighter Side of New England Agriculture," an address before the State Board of Agriculture, New Hampshire Reports, 1890, Vol. II. For an ampler statement see Professor Brewer's pamphlet, "The Farm and Farmer the Basis of National Strength," pp. 12-18.

sets the boy free by employing the machine, which neither eats nor acquires bad habits when idle. The community that loses its boys of ability may be impoverished, but the enrichment of the world is a compensation that stifles regret.

In the old times additional laborers were needed in the busy seasons. This irregular employment yielded an uncertain and scant living, which was eked out by tilling a little land, by chopping wood, and by working in other ways that were wasteful. When farmers now complain of the change in the labor supply, they are lamenting the disappearance from the community of families that furnished laborers at their call. These have gone, and their little houses have disappeared; but they have escaped the poverty that waits upon irregular employment, and the country town is relieved of a class that always was on the verge of destitution. The rural society that possesses mowing-machines is preferable to a social order that attempts to support men to swing a scythe a single month of the year. Even if wages advance, an agricultural community is richer without an impoverished working class. Machinery, which in cities creates social distinction, in the country works for social uniformity,—a condition more easily reached by the elimination than by the improvement of the weaker elements.

In the older parts of the country the observing traveller notes many an old cellar with its tangle of weeds and vines, or in field or pasture sees a clump of lilacs and straggling rose bushes,—enduring evidences that the spot was once a home,—or views with serious reflection a lonely shade tree lingering to preserve the memory of those who planted it. Sometimes a crumbling chimney still defies the winds, or a deserted house tells the tale of a vanished past. Some of these remains are silent witnesses of the lessened demand for labor since the machine came to the help of the farmer; many are the long lasting sign of "the abandoned farm."[1] These objects of much popular lamentation are found wherever sterile or rough land lies between fertile and easily tilled farms. They are more numerous in hilly than in level districts, in New England and New York than in the prairie states; but they mark a condition rather than a section. The new transportation did not open to settlement the distant parts of the country early enough to prevent a multiplying population from occupying land that is unfit for farming. In the age of homespun, conditions were so different that folly need not be charged upon those home makers who, at the worst, made a virtue of necessity and chose what remained after they arrived upon the scene. The spinning-wheel and the loom were as serviceable in the house beside the untravelled road that threaded the wilderness of hills and woods as on the rich estate; sheep throve in the wild pastures; the virgin soil yielded what was needful for food; neighboring farms offered employment when supplies were inadequate; the forest afforded means of barter in wood and shingles and lumber. It is possible to see how this fringe of unfortunate folk hanging upon industrially independent communities lived in part by

[1] Cf. pp. 66–69.

working for prosperous neighbors, in part by household industries, and in part by rude farming; and it is equally clear that changed conditions made existence on these small and poor farms impossible.

The day when the enterprising farmer began to produce for the market and to substitute machinery for hand tools, marked the doom of his unhappy neighbor hampered by inferior land. Machinery could not be used in his rough fields; it could not be employed profitably in mere patches of grass or grain; and besides capital was lacking for its purchase. The competition was hopeless; the support of an earlier time failing, the abandoned farm was inevitable. The escape of a stranded class is proof of vitality. These people have gone, but for the most part they went without suffering and without shame. A member of the family became a pioneer in the city, leading the way for brothers and sisters; at last the parents finished their earthly course, and the old home was left vacant. In many cases the abandoned land has been added to an adjacent farm to provide wood and pasture, so that the true interpretation of the decaying house by the hill-road is often to be found in the rich farmer's prosperity as he adds field to field, rather than in the poor man's poverty. Although its story is often read with a different emphasis, the abandoned farm really means the salvation of the family that forsook it, and the elevation of the community that is pruned of its least thrifty members. The unfortunate people on the poor lands forsook their impracticable homes before the development of wide areas of stagnation.

A thousand times better for civilization, is a thriving forest than a decaying humanity,—a rich pasture for improved cattle than a habitat for degenerate and hopeless men. "Out upon the doctrine," cries Professor Brewer, "that the country wants blooded stock, but a scrub race of men, on its farms. . . . Better let the lands be 'abandoned,' and stay abandoned; better let the forests grow anew and untouched, where the fox may dig his hole unscared, and the traveller lose his way in the wilderness, than that New England thought, New England culture and New England statesmanship, be turned over to a peasant class."[1]

It may be said of every phase of this industrial revolution, for it is nothing less, that its true interpretation finds elements of social progress. The country town is at a higher stage of civilization when its poor lands are abandoned; when its irregularly employed laborers have emigrated; when women are relieved of the wearing labor of spinning and weaving and butter-making; when sons and daughters of promise find alluring opportunities in a larger world. Yet such depletion is an exhausting strain, perilously disturbing the social structure; generations must pass before the adjustment to new conditions becomes a tradition as inspiriting as the memory of the " good old times."

The key to the change is the transfer of manu-factures to the factory. The factory creates the larger village, and the massing of factories develops the city, whose amazing growth is the distinctive feature of the nineteenth century. This city must have food from

[1] " The Farm and Farmer the Basis of National Strength," p. 30.

the country. The consequence is a new kind of farming for the market; production in one place for consumption in another, is the condition of trade; and trade demands transportation. Trade and transportation, in turn, call for new manufactories of rails and bridges and cars, for warehouses and offices; and these are located in cities, drawing the laborer from the country. He who lived precariously on the farm adds another to the consumers of the city, where, too, the owner of the abandoned farm thrives and demands his daily bread. Besides all those to whom the city gives prosperity, there is an uncounted multitude hovering on the brink of ruin, unable to gain a secure place in the new civilization, but requiring to be fed and by some means gaining the price of bread. Thus the city grows beyond all the experience of the race, and the country becomes a base of supplies for the city. Industrial independence of rural communities has gone forever: henceforth they are vital parts of the economic organism of the world. In this radical readjustment the farmer is helped by machinery, so that he widens his fields and intensifies his cultivation, and with less labor meets the new demand with an abundant supply. The age of homespun has given place to the age of machinery, and every element of life in the country town is changed.[1]

----

[1] This chapter and those that follow were written before the author had consulted Mr. Arnold Toynbee's Lectures on the Industrial Revolution in England,—fragments unfortunately of a great work projected by this rare scholar and philanthropist. The revolution he describes is that which we seek to trace; but he deals with an older civilization, which

had fully matured in 1760. The chief differences are a cumbersome inheritance of trade restrictions exchanged later for free competition; a tendency towards great estates for social and political advantage, threatening the extinction of the yeomanry; extensive household manufactures for the general market; the privilege of the poorer people in such common lands as remained unenclosed; and a much slower growth of the population. On the whole a less elastic people seems to have suffered severer changes in England than in America,— which may account somewhat for the rural depression which gives a pessimistic tone to much of the English writing on this subject. But agriculture in England is exceptionally unfortunate from foreign competition as well as from aristocratic land hunger. In spite of these grave differences there is one industrial revolution in England and in America.

CHAPTER II

THE RURAL PARTNERSHIP WITH CITIES

It is difficult to realize how rural the United States was one hundred years ago. This condition was specially notable in Virginia, where the system of large plantations prevailed, and foreign goods were distributed along the banks of her navigable rivers.[1] Mr. John Fiske states that when Thomas Jefferson entered William and Mary College in 1760, lad of seventeen though he was, he had never seen so many as a dozen houses grouped together.[2] As late as the beginning of the nineteenth century, when Virginia contained about one sixth of the population of the United States, her largest cities were Norfolk with 6,926 and Richmond with 5,737 inhabitants. In the North the urban development was greater, and yet in the entire country there were at that time but six cities having a population exceeding 8,000. The smaller New England cities, Bridgeport, New Bedford, Gloucester, Newport, Bangor, and Portsmouth, as they are to-day, are comparable to Philadelphia, New York, Baltimore, Boston, Charlestown, and Salem one hundred years ago.[3]

[1] John Fiske, " Old Virginia," Vol. II, pp. 206–210.
[2] *Ibid.*, p. 213.
[3] For population of cities of the United States since 1790, see Census

In 1900 there were in the United States 517
cities having more than 8,000 inhabitants. The
rapid growth of cities is even more conspicuous in
the Old than in the New World.[1] Greater London,
far advanced in the acquisition of her seventh million,
leads New York in the race, having gained in seven
decades half a million more people than now live in
the circle of cities at the mouth of the Hudson.
Greater Berlin keeps well in advance of greater
Chicago, in forty years increasing as many hundreds
of thousands as throng five populous counties at the head
of Lake Michigan.   Vienna gains a figure in the census
of 1890 which Philadelphia could not equal by pushing
her borders beyond three adjacent counties,—the last
half century yielding her a growth that would people
the Quaker City to the limits of the municipality.   St.
Petersburg with suburbs approximately equals Boston
combined with the neighboring cities.   Here the comparison breaks down, for there remain no American
competitors with Paris, just beginning upon the ac-

of 1850, p. liii, or Census of 1890, Pop., Vol. I, p. 571. The statement in the text follows the earlier table, which gives Philadelphia in
1800 a population of 69,403 instead of 41, 220 in the later table.

[1] For estimate of population of American cities with environs, see
World Almanac, 1902, p. 392.

For population of European cities previous to 1852, see Census of
United States for 1850, p. liii. For later statistics of European
cities, see Statesman's Year Book, " 1904," or World Almanac, 1903, p.
374. For critical review of statistics not later than 1897 and many
valuable tables, see " The Growth of Cities," by Adna Ferrin Weber, an
exhaustive and most judicious work, being the eleventh volume of
Studies in History, Economics and Public Law edited by the Faculty
of Political Science of Columbia University.

cumulation of the fourth million within the metropolitan district, and Constantinople, well established in the class of cities whose people are numbered with seven figures.

If we consider European cities of the second class, their number, their magnitude, and their recent expansion are alike imposing. Of cities having from four hundred thousand to a million inhabitants, the United States has only St. Louis and Baltimore, if Boston is placed in the class to which its environs raise it. In contrast with this paucity, Europe would be able to equip each state east of the Mississippi, except the four smallest, with a great city of this second grade. As we go down the list of European cities of the third grade, making one hundred thousand inhabitants the lower limit, we pass three such cities for every one in the American column. Many European cities have grown with extraordinary rapidity. If Cologne is compared with Cleveland for the decade after reaching a population of 160,000, if Lodz and Minneapolis are compared for the period since 1885, when the two cities were nearly equal, if Leipsic is set by the side of Chicago for the ten years before each city had 400,000 inhabitants, the result is a revelation to those who have been accustomed to boast of the unparalleled growth of American cities, for Cleveland and Minneapolis are outclassed, and Chicago and Cologne are so evenly matched that it is impossible to assign the honors without a detailed knowledge of suburban annexations.

At the beginning of the last century Europe as well

as America was comparatively rural, for it then contained no more than twenty-two cities whose population exceeded one hundred thousand. The sixteenth century saw such cities increase from six or seven in number to thirteen or fourteen; beyond that period Europe was virtually without cities, for after the decline of Rome, Constantinople was the only example in Europe of one hundred thousand people dwelling contiguously. Great cities are not exclusively a modern phenomenon, for Carthage, Rome, and Alexandria were comparable in size to St. Louis and Baltimore; and beyond the range of exact information, magnified doubtless in the tradition of immensity, were Thebes, Memphis, Babylon and Nineveh.[1] Ancient cities developing as political capitals and subsisting upon the spoils of conquest, afford important evidence of the strength of the gregarious impulse; but they rest upon an industrial system so radically unlike that of the modern era that they cannot be studied under the same principles as the cities of the present world. The same may be said of the vast agglomerations of population in China. In South America and in Australia, the urban movement is similar to that in the United States and in Europe, although the stage of development is reflected in the comparatively small number of great cities. Modern industrialism has so far influenced India and Japan that a new urban growth is beginning to appear, but it is quite impossible to distinguish the new centralization from the old density of population.

Great and growing cities are found wherever the new

[1] Weber, Op. Cit., pp. 448, 449.

industrial order has prevailed.   That their phenomenal development during the last hundred years is due to industrial causes, such as are suggested in the foregoing chapter, is sufficiently evident, although other causes in other ages have produced cities of vast proportions. For our purpose the comparison should be made with rural America and rural Europe of times just vanished, as historical epochs are measured, rather than with classic or oriental urban developments.   The age of cities stands in contrast with the age of home-spun.

This amazing rise of the cities must powerfully influence all rural communities.   We must now attempt to determine the nature of this influence.   Are the cities draining and exhausting the country, or do they admit the country to a fair and profitable partnership in one comprehensive movement of civilization.   First impressions, certainly, are misleading.   Thus it suggests that the rural population is in a state of decay, to say that from 1790 to 1900 it fell from 96.6 per cent. to 66.9 per cent. of the total population in the United States.   And when it is realized that one third of the people in the whole country dwell in cities and that already it has come to pass that the rural towns of Massachusetts contain less than a quarter of the population of that state, the impression of a stampede cityward is given.[1]   It is a fair use of such statistics when they are employed to arouse interest in the swift development of cities, but for the understanding of rural conditions

[1] Twelfth Census U. S., Vol. I, pp. lxxxii, lxxxiii.   Cf. Rev. Josiah Strong, D. D., " The New Era," Chap. VIII ; " Our Country," Chap. X.

it is necessary to observe more exactly what has happened.

The growth of the cities has been made possible by the natural multiplication of the population. It is true that the movement has been from country to city, but the city has scarcely absorbed the extraordinary increase of the race under modern conditions. Many rural districts are seriously depleted, as will appear in the following chapter, but the rural population as a whole is undiminished. Its partnership with the urban population in one economic enterprise assures its maintenance. It is a mistake of a too ready imagination to conceive a rural exodus leaving a mere remnant of the people in the country. A statistical demonstration of the error is not difficult, but before attempting that, it will be helpful to gain a clear understanding of the rapid multiplication of the human race under favorable conditions.

For the six decades from 1830 to 1890, the increase of the population of the United States by reproduction alone varies from twenty-eight to fourteen per cent.;[1] compounded decennially it amounts approximately to 225 per cent. for the entire period. If Massachusetts had not received an immigrant since 1830, in case she could have kept all her people, and they had increased at this rate, in 1890 she would have had only 255,000 less than her actual population. Under the same circumstances, Connecticut would have passed her actual figure in the census and have been

[1] "Statesman's Year Book, 1902," p. 1201. For the comparative fecundity of the native and foreign stocks, see Chap. IX.

able to make good the deficiency of Massachusetts lacking 35,000. Thus isolated New Hampshire could have reached the density of population attained in 1890 and with her surplus of half a million have filled a Boston where Portsmouth now stands. Vermont, at this rate, could have peopled her own towns, supplied a Boston on Lake Champlain, and have had 80,000 persons for a Worcester in the Connecticut valley. Maine also could have taken the record from her neighbors by some thousands in excess of their overflowing numbers. And if a Chinese wall had been built around New England so that no one could have entered or escaped, if this rate of increase had been maintained, these states could have provided people for all their growing cities and have furnished to a metropolis at Newport a million and a half of souls.

In Europe the natural increase of population is scarcely less startling. During the five years ending in 1900, Germany, Russia, and the Netherlands approximated an increase of seven per cent., which was the rate of the United States from 1885 to 1890; Austria and Hungary, Norway and Sweden, Great Britain, Belgium, and Italy did not fall far behind; and France hovered about the point of equilibrium, making an insignificant gain in four of the five years.[1] But the aggregates are more illuminating; during the five years Great Britain gained by natural increase two millions, Germany four millions, and Russia nine millions. It is plain from what source the vast urban populations are

[1] Computed from excess of births over deaths as stated in " Statesman's Year Book, 1902."

derived, and that it is quite possible for a country to develop great cities without depopulating the rural towns.

The new methods of food production have made possible an enlargement of population far beyond the point which was a necessary limit when Malthus propounded his doctrine in 1798. We may accept the judgment of David A. Wells that Malthus was entirely right from his standpoint on the economic conditions of his time, in asserting that the population of the world, and particularly of England, was rapidly pressing upon the limits of subsistence, and could not go on increasing because there would not be food for its support.[1]

Emerson has seized the essential point in the problem of population with characteristic acuteness: " It needs science and great numbers to cultivate the best lands, and in the best manner. . . . Population increases in the ratio of morality." [2]   If population is determined by subsistence, subsistence is a matter of intellectual and moral progress. The natural increase of the race tends to be somewhat in excess of the food supply, even when economic development has greatly enlarged it.   President Hadley, whose discussion of the doctrine of Malthus is singularly penetrating, correctly teaches that " the physiological possibilities of the birth rate are so far in excess of any death rate which is consonant with social prosperity

[1] " Recent Economic Changes," p. 330.
[2] " Society and Solitude," Farming, Riverside Ed., Vol. VII, pp. 146, 147.

that the improvement in the art of the food supply, direct or indirect, will not generally keep pace with this possible excess."[1]   The cities are the massed multitudes to whom modern conditions have given the boon of existence; their throngs are derived from the multiplication of a prolific stock without any necessity of robbing the country towns of their complement of people.   The city has taken the major part of the increase of population, but it has not reduced the aggregate of those who dwell in villages and on farms. The story of the statistics may now be rapidly told.

Russia is the European example of a vast and rapidly increasing rural population, corresponding most nearly to the United States.   According to Weber's tables, which are constructed with painstaking care, the rural population of Russia almost exactly doubled between 1838 and 1897.[2]   Here, as in France and Germany, the rural population consists substantially of the people dwelling in communities of less than two thousand.

At the opposite extreme is France.   Changes in territorial limits prevent the use of Weber's table for the whole period since 1846, when the census first made the distinction between the rural and the urban population.   The comparison is disturbed also by the concentration of troops resulting from the war with Germany.   There remain for our purpose the periods 1846–1856, 1861–1866, and 1881–1891.   These show losses of rural population,—the amounts being

[1] Arthur Twining Hadley, " Economics," pp. 41–51.
[2] Op. Cit., p. 107.

509,207 for the first, 124,831 for the second, and 543,-
606 for the third of these periods.[1] It seems probable
that the decline is continuous, though slight, since
1846. This accords with what has been said concerning the rate of natural increase in France.

Germany, in which we have noted an enormous
growth of cities, has a stable rural population. Weber's
table shows a rural loss in the empire of 34,111 from
1871 to 1890.[2] During the last decade there was a
rural loss of 237,289.[3] It is possible that this small
loss is apparent only, as many towns cease to be
counted on the rural side when they pass the limit of
two thousand inhabitants.[4]

England affords the distinctive illustration of the
urban tendency. In 1901 seventy-seven per cent. of
the population of England and Wales was urban. The
urban growth has been from less than nine millions in
1851 to more than twenty-five millions in 1901. Nevertheless the rural population probably remains undiminished. It is true that Weber's table shows a
rural loss of 829,779 from 1851 to 1891 ;[5] but during

[1] Op. Cit., p. 68.

[2] Op. Cit., p. 90.

[3] Computed from the rural percentages in the "Statesman's Year
Book for 1904," p. 665.

[4] The possibility of diminished returns of the rural population without actual loss is shown in the case of a decline in the rural population in New Hampshire from 1890 to 1900 of 20,804 (towns of less
than 8,000 inhabitants being classed as rural), while four towns which
had furnished 24,714 to the rural population in 1890 had grown out
of the rural class in 1900. For exact comparison the territory must
be the same.

[5] Op. Cit., p. 46.

that period a change in classification was made, and many towns outgrew the rural class. During the last decade the rural population made a gain of 151,649.[1]

The magnitude of the rural population and the rapidity of its increase in the United States are so impressive that only the most general statements need be made, although attention has been called to the decline in the rural percentage so repeatedly and so emphatically that the actual facts are much obscured. The distinction of the United States appears from the contrast with England and Wales. The urban populations of the two countries are not far apart, the United States having 30,583,411 people in towns and cities of more than 2,500 inhabitants in 1900,[2] and England and Wales having 24,639,556 in her towns and cities of more than 3,000 in 1901 ;[3] but while England and Wales approximate a rural population of eight millions in towns of less than 3,000 the United States exceeds forty-five millions in her towns of less than 2,500 inhabitants. The substantial and steady growth of the rural population of the great republic is most clearly shown in the aggregates for the several periods. The earlier arrangement of the census makes possible the following statement of the total population of towns and cities having less than 8,000 inhabitants :[4]

[1] "Statesman's Year Book, 1904," p. 19.
[2] Found only in Census Bulletin, No. 149, p. 23.
[3] "Statesman's Year Book, 1904," p. 19.
[4] Computed from Twelfth Census, U. S., Vol. I. p. lxxxiii.

1840	-	-	-	-	16,615,459
1850	-	-	-	-	20,294,290
1860	-	-	•	-	26,371,065
1870	-	-	-	-	30,486,496
1880	-	-	-	-	38,837,236
1890	-	-	-	-	44,349,747
1900	-	-	-	-	50,485,268

Although towns too large for the most satisfactory results are included in this table, it is worth noting that the rural population thus reckoned has nearly doubled since 1860, and that in 1880 it exceeded the total population at the preceding census, and that even in 1900 it was greater than the entire population two decades earlier. It may be added that more people were living in towns of less than 2,500 inhabitants in 1900 than were comprised in the total population of the country in 1870. Great and growing as are the cities, it should not be forgotten that three in five of our people still live on farms and in villages, or to be exact, that at the last census 59.8 per cent. of the people dwelt in towns of less than 2,500 inhabitants.[1] This immense rural growth is disguised, of course, by spreading over new lands, and it is to be explained by the fact that the United States furnishes a rural base of support not only for her own cities but for a portion of the cities of Europe.

The evidence clearly justifies the conclusion that cities may multiply and grow to an amazing extent without diminishing the rural population as a whole. Indeed France, with an abnormally low birth rate, is

[1] Census Bulletin, No. 149, p. 21.

the only clear case of rural depopulation which we have discovered,—and this is insignificant.

One who approaches these problems from the side of the city is justified in saying: " Each successive year is certain to see a smaller place for the workers of the world in the fields and on the farms, and a larger place in shops, counting-rooms, offices, banks, manufactories, and the myriad industries that make their home in the metropolis,"[1] if it is meant that the place of rural workers is relatively smaller; but as long as the multifarious business of the city deals with the materials derived from farm and forest and mine, and the staples of food are produced from the soil, it will be impossible for the actual place of rural workers to grow less from year to year. To say with this writer, " In the older states of the Union, the cities are draining the country in quite the European fashion,"[2] suggests a rural depopulation beyond the facts. We agree to the proposition, eloquently championed by Dr. Josiah Strong: " There is every prospect that for generations to come an ever increasing proportion of our population will be urban"; but we ask for further evidence when he adds, " We must therefore expect the steady deterioration of our rural population."[3] The needed discrimination is found in the guarded statement by Mr. John A. Hobson who dwells upon the smaller proportion of the people employed in extractive and domestic industries in advanced industrial

[1] Samuel Lane Loomis, " Modern Cities," p. 53.
[2] *Ibid.*, p. 27.
[3] " The New Era," p. 177. Cf. " Our Country," p. 138.

communities, but significantly adds that it is unlikely that this is so in the whole world.[1]

Country and city are united in an indissoluble partnership, which is equitable and for their mutual profit. The farms feed and clothe the urban millions, forests and mines furnish dwellings and indispensable mechanism; the city repays the service in honest work, which its mills and factories make efficient in the highest degree. So great is the advantage of costly machinery, that the city can take the toll of its maintenance and even of its wealth out of the traffic, and then return to the rural partner what he needs of his product wrought into the form for consumption that the highest civilization approves. It is true that the city thrives from its part in this interchange, for it supplies mechanical skill, commercial sagacity, expert superintendence, and technical knowledge,—all of which command high compensation. This talent for exchange, whose proper theatre is the city, handles the situation so ably and generously that in addition to his own grains, and meats, and fibres, passed through the processes of manufacture, the farmer receives for his labor furnishings and adornments for his home, books and papers for his instruction, and a liberal contribution to his bank account. The farm has a double significance for commerce, for from it are derived the materials of manufacture and trade, and to it return the rich products of the toil and skill of the city. The farmer's consumption is the base of urban prosperity as certainly as the city's need affords a market for the

[1] " Evolution of Modern Capitalism," p. 333.

product of the farms. Each partner is indispensable
to the other both as producer and as consumer; each
contributes its labor and each receives in the distribution of the final product. The massed wealth of the
city excites jealousy without reason, for it is the servant
of the farmer and on every occasion humbly acknowl-
edges its dependence. The chronic complaint of the
farmer that he is robbed by extortionate manufacturer
and merchant and carrier, is but the tradition from an
age when he divided with none the yield of his lands,
—living in peaceful but unprofitable industrial independence. Whatever increases the facilities of the
city, lowers its rate of toll charged upon the farmer.
The net result of civilization must be that less and less
is collected in the circuit from the producing fields to
the consuming household,—such being the significance
of lower freights, cheapened processes of manufacture,
and the economies of consolidation. The city is no
highwayman lurking by the route of traffic, but a
skilled magician multiplying all values. The wonder
of the age is that the farmer, who once carried his bag
of corn to the mill on the neighboring stream, can now
present all the fruit of his toil to the subtle alchemy of
the city and receive it back for his household transformed by modern invention and art, without violence
to his frugal conscience.

The growth of the city, therefore, assures a corresponding rural development and prosperity. Nothing
is more devoid of economic intelligence than the
representation of the city as growing continuously
through the gregarious instinct of men, until the

country ceases to be significant in comparison. Saying no more of the city as the servant of the farmer, it is worth while to dwell a little upon the vast and growing market for the produce of the farms which the multiplying and giant cities of the age afford. To a degree not often recognized, the cities of the old world are tributary to the prosperity of American farms. The annual average of agricultural exports of the United States for the five years ending June 30, 1900, was $752,120,133.[1] This amounts to $131 for each of the farms reported in the Twelfth Census, and this was a fifth of their gross income for the year 1899. This is in striking contrast with the entire absence of a foreign market in 1810, when the landed interest had no actual foreign purchasers for its wool, flax, hemp, hides and skins of domestic animals, and various metals, and there was no redundant raw material for cloth and furniture except cotton.[2] Agricultural exports, with the possible exception of cotton, are consumed chiefly in cities. If we assign two-fifths of the home consumption to cities, it becomes evident that approximately half of the products of our farms find a market in the requirements of the vast and growing urban population at home and abroad. The growth and prosperity of the city tend, first to expand the cultivated area, and afterwards to develop favored rural sections. The effect cannot be fully evident until

---

[1] Circular No. 23, U. S. Department of Agriculture, Section of Foreign Markets, p. i. The average for the three following years was one-sixth greater.

[2] Tench Coxe, Op. Cit., p. ix.

the virgin soils of the world are occupied, and the stimulus now dissipated to the ends of the earth is concentrated upon a region with fixed boundaries.

It is an interesting question whether the rural base is now large enough for the support of the cities. If the city outgrows the country, there is scant production for the demand, and high prices of farm products reveal the deficiency. Present prices suggest this condition. It is, however, so easy to trace the change in the price of many articles to the partial failure of the corn crop in 1901, that inferences concerning this special significance of prices are uncertain. Beef, pork, and milk responded when the average farm price of corn leaped from 35.7 cents in 1900 to 60.5 cents in 1901. Other conditions add to the perplexity of changes still in progress; it will be safer to gather evidence from a longer period.

Corn reached its lowest point from 1866 to 1901 in 1896, when the average farm price was 21.5 cents.[1] This was due, in part, to the exceptional crop, which was the largest during these thirty-five years, and in part, to special conditions, which will soon appear. Wheat fell to the lowest point during the same period in 1894, when the average farm price was 49.1 cents.[2] The crop in the United States was small, but the world's production was the largest up to that date. The exceptionally low price of these staples points to some cause more powerful than the magnitude of the

[1] " Year Book of the Department of Agriculture for 1901," p. 699.

[2] *Ibid.*, p. 709. Cf. George T. Fairchild, LL. D., " Rural Wealth and Welfare," pp. 87–91.

crops. This was the era of low prices in all lines of trade. A table prepared by the United States Department of Labor gives the average relative wholesale price of two hundred and fifty commodities for each of the years from 1890 to 1903.[1] The average for the first ten years of this period being 100, the range is from 112.9 in 1890 to 89.7 in 1897. Since the bottom of the decline was reached, the recovery has been rapid. The average stood at 112.9 in 1902—a striking coincidence—and at 113.6 in 1903. Farm products open in this same period at 110, fall to 78.3 in 1896, and rise to 118.8 in 1903. Beginning 2.9 points lower, they rise 5.2 higher than the whole list of commodities. The level of 1900 is almost identical with the level of 1890 in farm products, while it is 2.4 points lower for the entire list. The sharp rise in the price of corn and its consequences, noted above, contributed to the extraordinary advance of farm products culminating at 130.5 in 1902. Disregarding this, the whole period shows remarkable stability in agricultural prices, which gained 8.8 points while all commodities gained only 0.7 of a point. Such high prices of farm products at the close of a period of fourteen years, in the midst of which they were depressed 11.4 points lower than all commodities, seem to signify that the rural base is now barely sufficient for the support of the cities. The great depression in the prices of farm products at the middle of the last decade is explained by the

[1] Bulletin of the Department of Labor, No. 51, p. 248. For retail prices see *Ibid.*, No. 53, pp. 703-712. Also Josiah Strong, "Social Progress for 1904," pp. 74-76.

inability of the cities to make their customary pur-
chases during the hard times. Here we have the
proof of the delicate adjustment of country to city ;
in normal times it appears that the rural base is a
little too small.

To the maintenance of prices should be added the
fact of a new ratio of cereal production to population. The corn area increased 31.7 per cent.; the
corn production 25.6 per cent.; the wheat area 56.6
per cent.; and the wheat production 40.6 per cent.
during the ten years covered by the Twelfth Census.
The gain in population during the same period was
but 20.7 per cent. An enlargement of the supply
with no fall in prices indicates a growing demand.
In the case of wheat and corn, it is fair to say, prices
had received no unsettling shock from the increased
production before the close of the year 1903, although
the fluctuation in these staples is so great that inferences from their price in any single year would be
hazardous. Just how far the demand for wheat and
corn is due to growing cities is not clear, for one of
the striking changes of modern civilization is the
increase of bread-eaters, and important changes in the
feeding of stock have opened up new uses for corn.
Yet in one way and another rural prosperity seems
assured, and it is certain that the dominant factor in it
is the growth of cities.

The most significant index of the urban demand
upon the farms is beef. When the relative wholesale
price of corn went to 156.9 in 1902, the like price of
cattle rose to 139.5, and of fresh beef to 125.9. In

1903 these abnormal prices settled to 121.1 for corn, 105.8 for cattle, and 101.7 for fresh beef.[1] The rela tive retail price of beef fell more slowly from 118.5 —the highest point in the fourteen years covered by the table—to 113, for the same years.[2] At least four powerful influences tended to raise the price of beef in 1902—the high price of corn; the small number of cattle in the country; the general prosperity; and the increasing monopoly of the trade. Prof. J. W. Sanborn, who discusses the production of beef with careful discrimination,[3] attributes the high prices of recent years to the loss of neat cattle during the last decade. Unfortunately the change in the basis of enumeration in the Twelfth Census prevents its use in determining this point. Professor Sanborn approves the estimate that this loss amounted to from seven to nine per cent. from 1890 to 1900. In his view low prices at the middle of the decade checked production. This occurred at the critical moment when beef production was passing from the range to the farm owing to the withdrawal of large areas of grazing lands for settlement, the checking of the free use of land, the grazing off of surplus grass accumulated through many seasons, and the destruction of grass by the trampling and feeding of the herds. All conditions considered, it is remarkable that the price of beef did not gain and maintain a higher point. Consumption, doubtless, fell off as

[1] Bulletin of the Bureau of Labor, No, 51, pp. 267, 268.
[2] Ibid., No. 53, p. 707.
[3] " Agriculture of Massachusetts, 1902," pp. 61–79.

prices advanced, which hastened the return to a lower level. So far as one can judge in the midst of changes whose issue cannot be anticipated, it would appear that the present production of beef is not adequate for the hunger of the nation. Certainly there must be a radical change in this industry in the immediate future, as the cattle leave the ranges for the farms. The significance of this new development for the corn belt is clear, and it is possible that Professor Sanborn is justified in his contention that the time has come for New England to compete with the West in supplying beef to the cities.

Whether it will be possible under the new method of production to keep the price of beef within reach of would-be consumers, is still uncertain. The ultimate place of great masses of the people within or without the beef-eating class is one of the most interesting and important issues of industrial and social development. There is likely to be a new application of science to the feeding of stock and to the treatment of soils, in consequence of which the cost of production will be lowered, and it will be possible for those who have but average incomes to have this wholesome and necessary food upon their tables without extravagance. It is obvious how great a part in this social achievement must be taken by the distributing agency. By diminishing the cost of transfer from the farmer to the consumer, a monopoly may make the business on a great scale possible, or by exacting an exorbitant toll, it may arrest a great industry, with serious detriment to the strength and vitality of great masses of the people.

That such a power to injure and to help should be under governmental control needs no argument, provided it can be shown that government has the wisdom for such delicate and critical functions.[1] But while this problem waits solution, the farmer has the stimulating assurance that the hungry multitudes of the cities have appetites that exceed their purses. The adjustment by which the producers who are willing to labor, may be able to raise the dietary standard of consumers who shall pay for skill and toil, ought not to be beyond the intelligence of the age.

In general it appears from current prices that the farmer's part in the association with the city that characterizes the time, is not overdone. If this be the truth, it has special significance in view of the vast expansion of the rural population into new lands. For a generation the gratuitous distribution of public lands in the United States has tended to depress agriculture throughout the world. The Great Powers have ransacked the earth for virgin soils from which to extract subsistence for their growing populations. The richest parts of South America—barred from European exploitation—have passed swiftly under tillage. The more valuable parts of Siberia will be quickly utilized. Africa is ever the seat of problems, and no one can predict the course of coming history along her mighty rivers. The prospect is that for a time— and not a long time—virgin soils will suffice for the economic health of the world. Then will dawn a new era when vast cities of portentous magnitude will

[1] Cf. Chap. XV.

make their demand upon a limited area with results that no man can foretell. The problem of subsistence for these teeming myriads must be passed on to the science of that time. Meanwhile present indications are that the world has advanced within a decade from a state of agricultural overproduction to a condition in which city and country are in delicate equipoise, with many intimations of demands in the near future that will tax the resources of the farmer to the utmost. The shock of immeasurable competition from the ends of the earth brought great confusion into agriculture. That ominous condition has changed; the old is now so much vaster than the new that it fixes the terms of competition. The period of cheap production within the area of profitable commerce has passed. Remote regions of comparatively small producing power will not be able to depress the markets of the world, whose prices will be fixed by the cost of production under a stable agricultural system. The demand of growing cities must be met from a rural base having less and less possibility of expansion, with the result that lands will increase in value, and the farmer will enjoy increasing prosperity.

Already farms are selling at high prices throughout the older West, and costly schemes of irrigation are warranted by prospective profits. In the East the tide has turned; anxiety concerning "abandoned farms" has ceased; and the uplift of new times begins to be felt. Great sections of New England and the Middle States are fast becoming an urban tract, depending directly upon local markets in the cities. In regions near and remote the city is the farmer's hope. One tide of prosperity flows everywhere, enriching urban and rural population alike; and if this full sea recedes its ebb is marked equally in city and country.

We may rest upon the certainty that the gregarious tendency will keep the cities full and growing, for a social impulse swells the urban population even beyond the magnitude that can be traced to economic necessity. Many persons prefer the crowd of the city to the isolation of the country, even if they forego sanitation and privacy and comfort; they cannot be induced to leave the squalor of the slum for the sweet breath of the fields; the noisy street holds them by the very qualities that give offense to more refined tastes. At a higher level the advantages and attractions of the city are great. The popular preference is for the city rather than the country, and for the big city rather than the small city. Indeed the love of bigness is a modern mania, so that beyond reason the huge city is a powerful social force.[1]

The chief factor in this movement, however, is economic pressure rather than a distinctly social impulse. Men go to the cities because under the new conditions a less dense population can live in the country; by the same conditions other men are forced out upon new lands. Sometimes the movement is direct, and the farmer migrates to the frontier; usually the city acts as a social clearing-house. Every boy and girl not needed on the farm or in the village, resorts to the

[1] Cf. Chap. XIII.

city, which can receive one more, just as the clearing-house can charge up as many items as come in. Yet the balance must be preserved, and for the new citizen somewhere in the world there will be a new rustic. The removal to the city is made because that is the path of least resistance; for the same reason many stay in the city. Even if there is work in the country, men untrained in the operations of the farm are unprofitable laborers. Often the fields call in vain to crowds in the city clamoring for work. A horde of raw immigrants and the city's own surplus of men cannot recruit the rural force, for a fine manual training and a tradition of skill from father to son are lacking. The management of farms is even more beyond the training and ability of city-bred men. Under the economic pressure the human stream flows cityward, and only natural reproduction can keep the fountains full.

The social attraction and the economic compulsion combine to make the cities as large as possibility allows. This assured growth of cities affords an increasing stimulus of rural development. The checks of population being removed by modern invention and industrial organization, and " race suicide " being more remote than ever before, an expanding rural population answers the demand upon the soil. The farmer having a monopoly of the means of subsistence, holds the key to the situation. Occupying the base of support of modern civilization, the farmer is the residuary legatee of human progress. If either partner in the common enterprise has an advantage over the other, the benefit must accrue to the one who produces that without which the other cannot live. But a better conception is that of mutual dependence and of common prosperity.

CHAPTER III

THE EXTENT OF RURAL DEPLETION

THE inevitable consequence of industrial advance to an age of machinery is the depletion of many country communities. This reduction of the number of the people may be temporary; but unless other factors of the new order afford compensation, it must occur wherever the textile crafts have left the household, and the use of improved implements has displaced the farm laborer, and the village trades have suffered in competition with modern manufactures. This movement has been aggravated by the inability of the occupants of the smaller and poorer farms to gain a secure place in a system of exchanges in which the price of products is determined by more favored competitors. The severest strain coming at the moment of the city's superlative attraction, the result has been the abandonment of thousands of farms. The extent of this rural depletion has now to be considered.

Such a thinning out of agricultural communities is compatible with the growth of the rural population as a whole. It is essential to the understanding of this movement that it should be interpreted from the axiomatic position that the gigantic and growing cities of the new age require an expanding rural base of supplies. Australia, South America, Russia, Canada, and the United States have added mines and forests and cultivated acres to the world's available resources to an almost incredible extent within a few decades. The occupancy of new lands within our own national domain is a phenomenon of history comparable to the migration of peoples in primitive eras, but infinitely more significant because of the almost instantaneous subjugation of a continental wilderness to the highest civilization. Approximately half of the farms of the United States in 1900 were unknown to the census of 1870, and two thirds of them to the census of 1850. The farm is the permanent basis of civilization, and no conceivable change in the social order can diminish the rural population of the world.

It should be remembered, also, that within the area of depletion innumerable thriving and growing rural communities are found. If this fact is overlooked, worthless inferences will be drawn from statistical aggregates. It does not measure rural depletion to ascertain the loss in the total rural population, nor does it rebut the claim of depletion to show that the totals are maintained from decade to decade. The movement is complex; everywhere gain and loss are mingled. The growing town offsets the losing town in the statistics, so that the census of countries, states, and even counties may give no sign of a world-wide phenomenon.

The town is the proper unit for the study of changes in the rural population,—the county being so large that the actual depletion of towns distinctly agricultural is lost from sight in the statistics which include all rural towns, of which many make a steady growth, from causes akin to those that enlarge the cities. This encouraging development of country towns will be considered in the following chapter. Depletion is found in communities of certain types, and in those only. It is none the less real because it is local; it is far greater than appears at first view, being disguised in all statistical tables save those of towns.

Dr. Strong, whose studies of changes in population are of great value, has published a table in which it appears that of 25,746 townships in the United States 10,063 lost in population between 1880 and 1890.[1] We have been so accustomed to boast of the rapid growth of the nation that we are not prepared for the fact that at the time of this investigation two fifths of its civil divisions were demonstrably caught in a process of actual depopulation. The true explanation of this experience goes far to relieve the fear of impaired vitality, but a social change of such vast magnitude, however certain may be its place in a movement of progress, cannot be contemplated without anxiety, for it requires a readjustment taxing to the utmost the resources of an alert and sagacious people. That the transition from one civilization to another has not been made successfully in all cases, is evident from the lugubrious tales of a multitude of observers.

In the South the depleted counties are found only in isolated spots, for the plantation system, and the prolific Negro—who lacks the migrating instinct, and is at once too poor and too patient with poverty to

[1] "The New Era," p. 167.

seek a more favorable environment—change the social problem fundamentally. The newer regions, never having received full settlement under the old order, cannot be depleted; if such townships could be excluded from the table, the showing for the mature parts of the country would be startling in the extreme. This movement is conspicuous in New England, where during the decade in question 62 per cent. of the townships were more or less depleted. It is more evident in the rich Empire State, 69.5 per cent. of whose townships stand in the losing column. It is more surprising to find the states that contain no great areas of poor land falling into the same class, as is true of Ohio with 58 and Illinois with 54 per cent. of losing townships. In a state so recently settled as Iowa, 686 of 1,513 townships contained fewer people when these ten testing years had passed.

When we understand that alongside of the diminishing towns in all these states are growing communities, favored by location on railways, by small manufactures, by concentration of trade, by residential preferences, by proximity to cities, by changes in the character of agriculture, we infer that in all countries where the rural population as a whole barely maintains its numbers, there must be multitudes of depleted towns to offset the more thriving rural centres. Certainly local depletion appears in France; it is unmistakable in Great Britain; it cannot be absent in Germany. What we see of this movement in the United States must be interpreted as part of a world-wide industrial and social revolution.

Whether this series of changes has run its course to the end, can be told only by one who is equipped for prophecy. It is possible, however, to gain an opinion concerning present tendencies by comparing the last decade with its predecessor. It will be sufficient to examine a limited field, provided it is a fair sample of the whole. New Hampshire in the East and Illinois in the West may be taken as typical states ; being so unlike in history and resources, any common tendency they show may be properly regarded as the revelation of principles applicable to the whole depleted area.

In Illinois a simple count of the townships and precincts (not wards of cities) which lost population from 1890 to 1900, is a revelation to one who shares the traditional view of the growth of the West in every part. As the marks are placed at the names of the losing townships in this thrifty state, one comes to feel the tragedy of disappointed hopes. The mark of depletion may signify only a trifling fluctuation, and yet when all is summed up, the aggregate outflow of people from these diminishing communities is large enough to arrest the attention of the sociologist. This scrutiny results in a long list of 522 losing townships, or a little more than one-third of the whole number. This is not so bad as the impression it makes, for when the worst is said, a thousand and more growing townships are found in the same area. But the point of interest is the comparison with the result reached by Dr. Strong, who a decade earlier found 792 losing townships. The figures seem to indicate an arrest of the movement, but it must be remembered that there is a limit beyond which depletion cannot go. Such a limit seems to have been reached here and there in 1890, so that if we ask how many townships had reached the bottom of the decline, a considerable number can be described in those terms. Nevertheless as long as one-third of the expanse of the great Prairie State continues to lose its people, it cannot be said that the movement has run its course. It may be conjectured with some confidence that the end of the cycle will fall in the present decade, for it seems impossible that decade after decade can show these losses ; but the evidence of a new condition must await another census.

We turn to the smaller state for a more detailed investigation. According to Dr. Strong, 152 of 241 towns in New Hampshire lost population from 1880 to 1890. Ignoring a few unorganized townships we find that of 235 towns and cities, 132 lost population from 1890 to 1900,—all but one of these having less than 2,500 inhabitants at the last census. It may be confidently asserted, therefore,—the evidence in New Hampshire being slightly more striking than in Illinois,—that the tendency apparent in 1890 was not reversed in 1900.

Of the 103 towns and cities that gained population during the last decade, 78 are rural,—having less than 2,500 inhabitants. These increasing rural towns are scattered among the 131 losing rural towns. New Hampshire is no more conscious of decay than Illinois ; indeed, the traveller would see more of prosperity than of anything else, for the gaining towns with their thriving villages are on the highways of travel. In almost every case it is possible to trace the growth of villages to special causes. When marked upon a map, their exceptional character appears. They lie along the valleys, showing an adjustment to the railway; they are strewn thickly through the mountains, indicating the presence of great lumbering interests and suggesting the summer colony with its profuse expenditures; they make a fringe about Manchester, confirming our anticipation of intensive farming in proximity to a home market. Sometimes, also, a brick-yard or a small factory explains the increase. So manifest are these special causes of growth that the general proposition that purely agricultural towns are depleted, emerges from the investigation overwhelmingly demonstrated.

The difference between basing an inference upon the rural aggregates of the census and deducing it from the footings for the depleted towns alone, which one must make laboriously for himself, is all-important for our purpose. The 209 rural towns of New Hampshire, which had 192,434 inhabitants in 1890,[1] contained only 185,319 inhabitants in 1900,[2]—the loss being 7,115. If Gilford, of which a large part was annexed to Laconia, is omitted, the rural loss is reduced to 4,191. But when the losses of the 130 depleted rural towns are summed up separately, they amount to 12,864, which is 11.4 per cent. of their population in 1890. If three larger towns which ex-

[1] Computed from the statistics of population.
[2] Twelfth Census Bulletin, No. 149, p. 23. Table not in Vol. I.

perienced an exceptional decline, are omitted on the ground that the loss was in the villages and had no relation to agriculture, it appears that the depletion of rural population within the losing area was approximately ten per cent. It is convenient to know, also, that the seventy-eight growing rural towns increased approximately ten per cent. during the same interval. As the causes of industrial and social change are everywhere of a like nature, it may serve as a convenient hypothesis that rural depletion from 1890 to 1900 was somewhat less than ten per cent. Doubtless it was greater in the East than in the West, but it was great enough East or West to strain rural society.

In general the middle of the last century marks the beginning of the ebb of population in rural towns of the depleted class. This obviously applies only to regions fully settled at that period,—culmination being later in a new state like Illinois than in such an old state as New Hampshire. It will suffice for our purpose if we can measure the duration and extent of rural depletion where it has had full opportunity. Rockingham County in New Hampshire received its first white inhabitants in 1623. Its situation, its resources, and its prosperity make it a not unfair representative of the older agricultural districts. Though surrounded by cities, it is itself distinctly rural,—the city of Portsmouth with 10,637 inhabitants being the only instance of a contiguous population exceeding 5,000. Of the thirty-seven towns in this county twenty-three had their greatest population in 1860 or earlier; of the others only six contained more people in 1900 than ever before. The twenty-three towns whose decline dates from 1860 or earlier have lost one quarter of their greatest population. Twenty-five per cent. in half a century may be regarded as the standard of depletion, exceeded here and there, approximated throughout wide areas, but inapplicable where the conditions are altered essentially by the shortness of the period of settlement.[1]

These local measurements are mere tests of our generalization. Nothing could be more rash than the assumption that a rate of depletion in one small state, or a single county of that state, measures the loss throughout the depleted area, and certainly one would not think of carrying this measuring line across the sea. Nevertheless just as there is a standard pound under the law of gravitation whether it be in England or Massachusetts or Iowa, so under the action of universal forces there is a standard rural depletion in the Old and the New Worlds alike, in France and New Hampshire and Illinois. And just as everywhere a pound weight may be lifted by whatever has the requisite strength, so under the social law of depletion the standard loss may be overcome by other forces. The downward pressure is everywhere the same, but the actual falling is arrested variously. To attempt to estimate this standard tendency of population under the new order of civilization may be rash; but for the help of the imagination, if nothing more, the conjecture may be

[1] In Massachusetts four towns in Hampshire County culminated in 1810: nine towns in Franklin County in 1820: and six towns in Hampden County in 1800. *Hampshire Gazette*, Sept. 10, 1899.

hazarded that the typical town representing the depleted agricultural population has experienced a loss of twenty-five per cent. of its people in fifty years.

It is difficult to conceive causes that can protract this movement many years. It would seem that the transfer of household industries to the factory was completed long ago, and that no further reduction of population from that influence can occur. It is almost as clear that the displacement of the agricultural laborer by machinery has run its course. If one looks with the utmost care for possibilities of further depletion, none appear throughout great sections. We are tempted to conclude that the rôle of the prophet is not too difficult for human reason reflecting upon these problems, but before indulging the prophetic impulse we must consider two factors that entail some uncertainty. Further depletion is not to be feared except where farming is unprofitable from the infertility of the soil or the smallness of farms. We may venture the hazards of prophecy when we have come to a conclusion concerning the future rôle of the " abandoned farm," and when we can determine whether there is likely to be a consolidation of petty farms.

By 1890 the abandonment of farms had become so common as to provoke much popular interest. The census of that year brought out an alarming evidence of what had been going on under the eyes of innumerable observers, for a loss of five million acres, of which four fifths was improved land, was recorded of the farms of the North Atlantic States,—every state in the division sharing this decrease. Several state legislatures were aroused, and state boards began to investigate the matter. In the year named the Massachusetts Bureau of the Statistics of Labor collected from the town assessors, reports showing the existence of at least 1,461 farms which they assigned to this class. Of these 689 were without buildings. The work was taken up by the State Board of Agriculture, which from first to last and by various methods secured information concerning 2,249 farms that came within the scope of the movement, although in some instances they were not actually without occupants. Seven hundred and forty-six descriptions of farms were supplied by their owners for publication. The first catalogue contained 328 descriptions of farms offered for sale, of which the average size was 115.55 acres, and for which the average price asked was $1,675.78. The ninth catalogue, published in 1901, contains 145 descriptions. Three hundred and thirty-one catalogued farms have been reported sold. The net outcome of this protracted and determined effort seems to be that some hundreds of farms in Massachusetts are known to be unoccupied; that comparatively few owners of such farms care to have their property listed in the published catalogues; that sales of these lands are frequent; and that few, if any, farms are now on the market for less than their actual value.[1]

The agitation concerning abandoned farms reached the New Hampshire legislature in 1889. A commissioner of agriculture and immigration was appointed,

[1] Descriptive Catalogue of Farms in Massachusetts, Ninth Edition.

who succeeded in securing reports from the selectmen
of 212 towns.   One thousand three hundred and forty-
two abandoned farms were reported,—farms without buildings and farms operated by the occu-
pant of an adjoining farm being excluded.   Only
fifty-eight towns claimed to have no abandoned farms ;
the largest number found in a single town was twenty-
seven.[1] From the beginning much was made of the
opportunity for summer homes amid the beautiful
scenery that often gives æsthetic value to these infertile lands.   Many abandoned farms have been pur-
chased for summer residences, of which there were
known to be 2,300 in the state in 1904.[2] This demand in addition to reoccupancy for farming has reduced the deserted area.   Even during the year subsequent to the date for which information was first collected, 141 of the reported farms were sold, and 160
were reoccupied by tenant or owner.

Other states have shown similar enterprise,—notably
Vermont, which was earliest in the field.   These vigorous measures taken at a time when a more hopeful
outlook and a movement into the country from the
city favored them, seem to have turned the tide.
Nothing, however, can change the fact that the poorest
lands ought not to be tilled as farms until the pressure
upon agricultural resources shall be greatly increased.

[1] " Annual Reports of New Hampshire, 1890," Vol. II, pp. 470–478.
[2] " New Hampshire Farms for Summer Homes," Second Edition.
The most complete collection of " abandoned farm " literature in existence is that made by Mr. Frederick H. Fowler, First Clerk of the
Mass. State Board of Agriculture.

Repeopling the depleted area to its former density is at present neither possible nor desirable. Though many other farms will be abandoned temporarily, and some farms permanently, the opinion seems warranted that the movement under alarming headway a decade or more ago has been arrested, and that depletion of the rural population by actual flight from the soil in days to come is a negligible quantity in the calculation of the development of country towns.

Some of the gravest rural problems grow out of the unprofitableness of small and infertile farms, which do not share the changed prospect of agriculture resulting from the growth of cities. Abandonment of such farms is an easy and wasteful rather than a wise and economical treatment of the difficulty. Consolidation of small and poor farms is a better solution of the problem. It is necessary to see precisely what the fundamental difficulty is.

In the *Forum* for November, 1892, Professor R. Means Davis of South Carolina College, felicitously points out the root of the trouble, as he observed it at the South. He regards the farm as burdened with a fixed charge of the family, amounting to four hundred dollars per year. If the farm yields forty bales of cotton, a profit of ten dollars per bale provides for the family at the average rate. The minimum farm, therefore, should have a capacity of forty bales of cotton, or an equivalent in supplies or salable crops. A farm too small for this production is the source of chronic hardship, and a country thus cut into fragments cannot escape poverty. Such is the explanation of the

impoverished farmer's condition offered by this suggestive writer, whose purpose is to expose the folly of
denouncing railroads, factories, and banks, and to
show the inevitable limits of " legislative lotions and
political panaceas." His advice is that such farmers
should endeavor to leave the production of staple crops
to large planters and devote themselves to " small
farming."

It is a sound principle that the fixed charge of the
family should determine the minimum size of farms.
The number of acres, of course, is not so important as
the scale of production. If the farm yields but half
the fixed charge of the family, its productivity should
be doubled; this may be done by a more intensive
cultivation or by an increased acreage according to
conditions. The question now in hand is this—Is the
enlargement of farms so evidently advantageous and
necessary as to make probable further depletion of the
least profitable agricultural districts ?   Certainly a definite fixed charge must be spread over a suitable earning area, and if this cannot be done, in case the income
from the farm cannot be supplemented by outside
earnings, there is no escape from grinding poverty.

It is not easy to determine the fixed charge of the
family on the farm in accordance with a wholesome
standard of living.   Three hundred dollars in addition
to fuel, food products, and house rent, would be comparable to six hundred dollars in money, and a farm
of this capacity may serve as a base line for our purpose.   Wherever farms are found which do not yield a
net cash income of three hundred dollars per year,

some form of consolidation is required for comfortable living and social health. In New England the convenient measure for farms is the number of dairy cows that can be kept on them. A farm with forty cows is considered a large farm. Such a farm will support a family at the rate of the fixed charge here specified, meet all expenses, and pay four per cent. on a valuation of from eight to fifteen thousand dollars. A community of farmers equipped on this scale has all the elements of comfort and thrift. If these same farms are divided and subdivided, the process cannot go far before the net cash income of the farmer is reduced to less than three hundred dollars. When that point is reached, the land gives nothing but an opportunity to work for a living, such as any mechanic enjoys. The land, therefore, ceases to yield a profit, and its value disappears. A certain size is necessary that farms may be tilled at a profit. Ordinarily if fertile farms were divided and subdivided, there would be compensation in a more intensive cultivation. In the case of poor lands intensive agriculture is impracticable, and there is no relief from an inadequate base of support for families except in additional acres. Just as rich lands may be made worthless by dividing them into small farms, so poor lands sometimes can be made profitable by consolidating them into large farms.

The form that consolidation may take is the subject of much interesting speculation. A citizen of New York, writing of these unprofitable farms, suggests consolidation with an owning corporation, allotments of stock to former owners, an expert manager, a new

grouping of residences, and a resulting social development.[1] Another writer advocates great pasturages for
sheep and cattle, with extensive creameries attached,
conducted somewhat on the plan of ranches in the
West.[2] Another plan is for a syndicate of farmers to
take up a thousand acres at a time in these poor sections, and bring to bear upon this large area concentration, organization, intelligent connection with markets, and quick capital. Doubtless there is here a
field for the theorist, and on paper the economies of
combination after the methods in manufacturing have
an attractive appearance. It may be doubted, however, that such schemes as these will ever prove practicable. Farming can never be put in charge of corporations working on the great scale, whether lands be
rich or poor ; and least of all can this be done where
the soil is unpromising. It is a provision of nature
that farming is most successful when the farmer's family occupies the land, and he calls to his assistance only
those laborers whom he can personally direct.

Our more modest suggestion is that the poorest
farms be annexed by purchase to adjacent farms, and
that they be allowed to revert to woodland and pasture ; that farms of a slightly better grade be combined
as the more thrifty farmer shall be able to buy out his
neighbor ; and that men of a certain kind of practical
ability, seeking opportunity for investment, put their
capital into as many farms as can be conveniently
consolidated, either conducting the enterprize them-

[1] *Berkshire County Eagle*, Jan. 23, 1890.
[2] *Boston Herald*, Dec. 24, 1889.

selves or renting the property to a competent farmer.
The opportunity for this readjustment lies in the long
subsidence of land values, now checked, it may be,
but in the case of poor and small farms halting at a
point where interest charges can be easily met. The
depreciation of land has gone so far in New England
that after checking off past losses, there is an equalization between the East and the West. The earning
capacity of western lands is now recognized, and
recent sales at high prices have fixed the interest
charge at so high a rate as to severely tax the resources of the soil. As long as great tracts of rich
land could be obtained in the West at nominal prices,
equalization between the productive and the sterile
farm was found in the distances from market. Now
with the development of railroads and the lowering of
freights, and with the growth of great cities in the
interior, the distance from market is less significant,
and the eastern opportunity in competition is in the
cheapness of lands as contrasted with high values at
the West. It is a fair question whether a large farm
in the East, operated in the modern way, cannot compete with the western farm of like value,—the larger
acreage being a compensation for the poorer soil.

It is frankly conceded that writers upon agriculture
uniformly recommend a better cultivation rather than
an increase of acres. The popular feeling distinctly
favors the small and thoroughly tilled farm. Intensive
farming offers the chief line of advance, but when it
has done its utmost, it cannot avert financial disaster in
those infertile sections that demand the consolidation

of small farms. An appeal to the census results in slight confirmation of such a tendency as we may venture to set down among the facts of the rural world. This is to be expected, for the zone of intensive farming must contain an increasing number of small farms, and if consolidation were well under way within its proper sphere, the fact would not appear in the averages of the census. Comparing the average size of farms in 1850, 1880, and 1900, it appears that in Massachusetts, where the urban influence is most evident, there has been an unbroken decrease in the size of farms; in Connecticut, first a decrease and then an increase; in Maine, which is the most distinctly rural, a continuous increase; in Vermont and New Hampshire, a small decrease and then a slightly larger increase. Since 1880 the tendency towards consolidation is distinctly manifest outside the area of intensive cultivation. Even in Illinois, where the richness of the soil alters the terms of the problem, the scale turned slightly towards larger farms in 1880. The summary for the entire country seems to indicate the discovery in the last two decades that the farm must be large enough for the fixed charge of the family, for in 1880 the average farmer had the smallest farm of the half century, to which he added three acres in 1890 and ten acres more in 1900.

It may be conjectured that in 1880 the patriarchal division of farms gave place to the economic consolidation of them. The repeated division of land produces an impoverished peasantry. The system has never prevailed in America as in some parts of Europe, for vast areas of virgin soil calling for occupants have served us better than a law of primogeniture at the time when our social order was plastic. We have now escaped the danger altogether, for it can never become the custom for children to settle upon a portion of their father's farm, until conditions are radically altered. The size of farms will be determined by economic considerations rather than by sentiment and by probate courts. They will be large enough, when we are as prosperous as we ought to be, to provide support for a family by the modern standard of living; whether they contain three or three hundred acres will depend upon the kind of farming to which they are adapted.

We are not able, therefore, to affirm that all signs point to the cessation of the rural exodus in the near future, for certain limited sections are not depleted to the point of the best economic adjustment. The significance of the remainder of this cycle of change is not great for any bearing that it has upon rural life in the aggregate, but it is considerable as it involves the welfare of many communities that have not yet passed through the severest strain. Social problems in the country are most acute where depletion is greatest, and the worst is not yet; but this worst will be limited territorially, and it will develop slowly. For many years to come there will be enough of these communities first condemned to poverty by overpopulation, and then shaken in every part of the social constitution by depletion, to provide those visions of decadence, which, whether they allure or alarm, easily

win the place of thrilling interest in current literature.

In the main rural depletion is over. In its whole
course it has been an adjustment of industrial necessity
and of economic health ; everywhere it is a phase of
progress and lends itself to the optimism that discerns
deeper meanings. Nevertheless depletion has gone
so far as to seriously affect all rural problems within
the area of its action. Were it not for this loss of
people, the development of country towns would
be along straight lines easy to trace. The difficult and perplexing problems are found where the
people are reduced in number. That broad, though
irregular, belt of depleted rural communities, stretch-
ing from the marshes of the Atlantic shore to the
banks of the Missouri, which have surrendered from
ten to forty per cent. of their people, within which
are many localities destined apparently to experience
further losses, calls for patient study of social forces
and requires a reconstruction of the whole social
outfit. But it should be remembered that an increasing population gathers in rural towns thickly strewn
throughout the depleted tract, and that the cheer of
their growth and thrift is as much a part of the rural
situation as the perplexity incident to a diminishing
body of people. To these increasing and improving
towns we must now give attention.

CHAPTER IV

THE ZONE OF RURAL GROWTH

ONE peculiarity of the rural problem—baffling to him who would solve it, but keeping alive the interest in it—is the strange contradictoriness of testimony. Every now and then some explorer retells the tale of the wilderness creeping in upon the farms, or a reformer turns his search-light upon some obscure community which for the moment startles the observer of its degeneracy. Yet every one knows country towns that afford scant material either for the sensational reporter or for the social alarmist. Familiarity with prosperous villages and happy rural populations, which is almost coextensive with memory and travel, prevents this pessimism from becoming a popular mood; indeed there are sparks of resentment when the mind accustomed to other observations is struck sharply by the unwelcome story of decay. This sense of misrepresentation assures attention to each new exploiter of the theme, and thus the discussion runs on with no end of pertinent facts that fail to carry conviction.

The explanation of this refusal to be convinced by unquestionable testimony is so simple that none ought to overlook it—there is a zone of depletion, perhaps of degeneration, and there is a zone of growth. Generalization is so powerful an instinct of the mind that one

contemplating the zone of depletion boldly proclaims
his discovery of the rural condition, and another familiar
with the zone of growth confidently challenges the
pessimistic interpretation of rural development.   As
in all such cases, the fault is not in the particular
observation, but in the unjustifiable inference from it.
The broad belt of rural depletion extending across
the states once fully settled is distinctly a zone.   Even
where depletion does not actually appear, the forces
that cause it are active, being overborne locally by other
influences.   For our thought, there is also a zone of
growth made up of all towns in which the new prosperity triumphs.   These towns may be scattered, they
may alternate with losing towns ; yet for our purpose
they constitute a zone of thrift and progress.

The student of rural problems should be able to
keep his mind clear by assigning facts as they come
into view to one or the other of these zones.   The
sensational tales of rural degeneracy, pruned of extravagance, are a perfectly consistent consequence of
forces everywhere at work ; they have their place in
the zone of depletion, in some parts of which deca
dence has exceptional illustration.   The sensational reporter and the screaming reformer deal chiefly with the
débris of a vast social movement ; to deny the facts they
allege in argument or present in picture, is no part of
the duty of the one who would be as optimistic as the
truth.   The thinning out of the rural population, however, which may have disastrous consequences, must not
be confounded with inevitable degeneracy.   " Most persons think," says Aristotle, " that a state in order to

be happy ought to be large; but even if they are right, they have no idea what is a large and what a small state. For they judge of the size of a city by the number of the inhabitants; whereas they ought to regard, not their number, but their power. A city too, like an individual, has a work to do; and that city which is best adapted to the fulfillment of its work is to be deemed greatest."[1] This is a sound principle; in general the depleted town has the number of inhabitants required for its work, and it is better off with the smaller number. Superfluous people are no sign of social health, and a lean and thin community is not to be set down as sickly in any intelligent diagnosis. On the other hand one should be able without hesitation to assign to the zone of growth the facts that belong there, and to interpret them in accordance with the movement of which they are a part.

In spite of all diligence, a false impression can scarcely be avoided, for human nature inclines to pessimism. If, for example, it is said that in a county of forty towns nineteen are losing population, the impression is that the county is in a bad way; yet the real fact is that a majority of the towns have an increasing population and are happy in the thrift that makes such growth possible. It is not as if the losing towns were the symptom of an unsound condition of the whole body. If nineteen fortieths of the human body were diseased, the whole body would be sick, but it is not so in a county of forty towns. If depletion were to be conceived as sickness, even then

[1] "The Politics of Aristotle," Jowett, Vol. I, p. 214.

there would be no occasion to regard the growing towns as endangered. But to keep to the point in hand, why should a minority of losing towns give the tone to opinion, and a majority of growing towns contribute nothing to the impression made? If of 25,746 townships in the United States 10,063 lost population from 1880 to 1890,[1] the fact is important and, perhaps, ominous; nevertheless the 15,683 townships that gained population ought to have some part in the composite impression, and who can say how great a part they would have, if once we were rid of the pessimistic tendency? When stated with the right aspect to the front, the facts have a hopeful look. In New Hampshire, a representative eastern state, only a little less than one half, and in Illinois, a typical state of the older West, about two-thirds of the townships are gaining population. There is much beside exact truth in human speech; there is also the impression with which it is freighted. In this case the optimistic or the pessimistic impression is the chief thing. We may say confidently that the declaration of growth makes the right, and that the assertion of depletion makes a false impression. In every part of the country there is much wholesome rural growth. If this zone of growth received a part of the attention that has been given the zone of depletion, there would be a fairer judgment of the rural situation.

The enlargement of the rural base of support for cities may be secured for a time by the subjugation of wild lands in new regions of the earth, but the

[1] Cf. p. 59.

force that drives the farmer to the far frontier finally finds another path offering less resistance. The supplies demanded by the city may be secured more cheaply from lands near at hand by an intensive cultivation. Or to approach the matter from another side, a farmer seeking to adjust the fixed charge of the family to an ampler base may double his production either by buying out his neighbor, or by changing his tillage of his own soil. In one set of conditions, the best policy will be the consolidation of farms ; in other conditions it will be wiser to double the production without increase of acres. The pressure of the cities upon the farms is already so powerful as to develop intensive cultivation in favored localities. Wherever this occurs, additional labor is demanded ; families are broken less frequently by son or daughter seeking employment elsewhere ; and here and there a small farm is set off, and a new family established in the neighborhood. All this shows in the census in increased population. In the future the growth of cities will continue ; their requirements will not be met by the opening of new lands to settlement ; pressure upon existing farms will become more sensible. The result must be a stimulus to intensive farming and a decided improvement of many country towns. This change appears throughout what we have termed the zone of growth.

By intensive farming many things are meant ; here any method of farming which increases production without adding to the acreage is intensive farming in the sense under consideration. The most available case for illustration is market-gardening. Somewhere in the country are grown the vegetables consumed in immense quantities in the city; and just so far as this new and rapidly expanding production extends, there is intensive farming of a radical kind. A few acres tilled as a garden require the labor that would find employment on a large farm cultivated in the common fashion. The income corresponds to labor expended rather than to acreage. Often the new is united with the old mode of farming, as when a strawberry bed, or a patch of pease, or a field of tomatoes is maintained without modifying the remainder of the farm. Proximity to a city, or even to a canning establishment, gives the necessary opportunity. Incidental profits of a like kind from orchards and from poultry may easily equal the revenue from the rest of the farm. As cities multiply, and gain immensity, there must be corresponding enlargement of the more incidental products of the farm; and here is great opportunity for the expansion of business without increase of acres.

The possibilities of the minor products of the farm appear when we place the several items side by side. The value of the wheat crop reported in the Twelfth Census was $369,945,320; poultry and eggs amounted to $281,178,035; vegetables, including potatoes and sugar beets, yielded $238,846,908 ; orchard products were worth $83,751,840. It requires no prophet to forecast the course of relative production in which the wheat farm will have a lower place than the market-garden and the poultry-yard. If small fruits were

classed with orchard-products, a third competitor
would show formidable strength. The diversification
of products is one of the most encouraging signs of
agricultural prosperity ; it points towards a denser
farming population and goes far to account for the
zone of growth.

Dairying and the rearing of animals for meat on
farms have large significance in this connection. The
crops taken from the soil are converted into higher
values with increased expenditure of labor. With a
given acreage, it is possible to increase the herds by
the purchase of grain and fertilizers ; as the herd
grows, the land gains in fertility. Doubling the
capacity of the land is better than doubling the
acreage, profitable as that may be in many cases.
The increase in the use of artificial fertilizers, amounting to 42.4 per cent. in ten years, averaging ten dollars
per farm in 1899, is evidence of a strong movement in
the intensive direction. As the farm takes the place of
the ranch in stock-raising, this movement will be accelerated. It is easy to see that when in years to
come cities approach their maximum size, their pressure upon the sustaining farms will force them to
maximum fertility.

The possibility of increasing the product by tillage
and fertilization is well illustrated by the yield of corn
per acre in the various states of the Union. No cne
for a moment will think that the soil of New England
can be compared with the soil of the corn-growing
belt of the Middle West, yet in the table showing the
yield of corn per acre from 1892 to 1901, the New

England states head the list year after year. Of forty records for the four northern New England states, not one falls below thirty bushels per acre, and fifteen records exceed forty bushels. In the entire table there are only two records of forty bushels per acre outside of New England; and the four states, Ohio, Indiana, Illinois, and Iowa, have sixteen records of less than thirty bushels in a total of forty records. It is a long way from 23.45 bushels to 38.06 bushels, yet that distance measures the difference between the average yield in the United States and the average yield in Massachusetts for the same years.[1] The uncertainties of the season are less in New England, and some allowance must be made for the failure of crops under less favorable climatic conditions; but it would seem to be practicable to increase the yield of corn fifty per cent. by intensive cultivation, adding a billion bushels to the crop without enlarging the acreage. Such costly tillage is not profitable until a market develops near at hand. The value of an acre of corn in Massachusetts for the ten years of the table here cited makes a total of $212.96, as compared with $92.14 for the same in Illinois.[2] Evidently the higher price stimulated more thorough cultivation. The corn raised in Massachusetts was consumed on the farm,[3] along with much more that was brought from the West. It had exceptional value because the animal products into which it could be converted commanded high prices in a region thickly strewn with cities. The neighbor-

---

[1] "Year Book of Department of Agriculture for 1901," p. 700.
[2] *Ibid.*, p. 701.　　　　　　　　　　　[3] *Ibid.*, p. 699.

hood of the city thus directly fosters intensive farming even in the production of cereals.

The reference to Massachusetts suggests a distinct phase of the subject. Around every large city is a group of suburban communities, many of which are distinct political units,—the larger being cities, the smaller being country towns. They grow and thrive with the growth of the city of which they are a part industrially and socially. They belong to what may be termed the urban tract. Under that designation might be included also such towns as receive a decided stimulus from the city market other than that which is distributed over wide areas. So efficient is the railway service that towns at a considerable distance, whose agriculture is shaped by urban customers, may be as really a part of the urban tract as a district within the city limits; other towns within the same radius may follow the ordinary methods of farming, and they would not belong to a true urban tract, however near they might be to cities. It accords with this last observation that Massachusetts contains many losing towns, of which some are in the near neighborhood of cities,—the whole state by no means as yet being an urban tract.

As a civilization more and more dominated by cities develops, the urban tract will grow in significance; it will constitute a considerable part of the zone of rural growth, although by a stricter classification it should not appear in the rural problem at all. It is a most interesting question to what extent an urban tract will transform the country adjacent to cities. It is possible that some change in the application of power will carry many manufactures into the country, just as the trolley has made it possible for multitudes to have homes in the suburbs. This, however, concerns the transformation of cities rather than changes in the rural condition; but it is worth noting that when the population reaches its maximum, in all probability the urban tract will be conspicuous and influential, touching rural life far more vitally than the congested city of an earlier time.

More to the point is the thrift of small cities and villages, which distribute the urban stimulus and powerfully influence adjacent farming towns. Weber considers that the centralization of manufactures reached its height in 1890.[1] He predicted that the Twelfth Census would show an exodus of manufacturing industries from the great cities. Causes for such a change, he found in high rents and taxes, and in the oppressive organization of labor in large cities. The equalization of freights by which all towns within a prescribed zone share the advantage of the metropolis promotes this tendency. The movement is into the suburbs, the small towns, and even the open country. This very careful student of industrial development looks for the covering of the country with industrial villages built up around one or two immense factories; but he does not believe that villages can retain this simple type, since allied industries will be attracted, and the village will grow into a city. The decisive factor in the location of manufactures would seem to

[1] Op. Cit., pp. 202–209.

be the supply of labor; flight from labor troubles in the city incurs other difficulties scarcely less serious in the country. Men prefer to work where they can pass easily from one factory to another, and they are slow to put themselves in the control of a single employer. And to this prudential wisdom, must be added the general reluctance to leave the more interesting life of the city for the duller experiences of the country. If one may judge from the operations of land and improvement companies, industrial migration is suburban rather than rural.

The fact of chief significance is the power of resistance of the small city and the larger village to the forces of concentration. The Twelfth Census presents facts concerning the localization of manufactures[1] that are somewhat surprising in view of recent developments in trusts and other mammoth enterprises. As would be expected each of the leading manufactures is entrenched in a few cities; the surprise is that so vast manufactures are still distributed outside of these centres. Thus the manufacture of boots and shoes is concentrated in fifteen cities of 20,000 or more inhabitants; cotton manufacture in twelve such cities; and the iron and steel business in ten cities. The form of statement varies, but it appears that in the boot and shoe manufacture, 41.8 per cent. of the total value of products for the United States for 1900 was reported from places of less than 20,000 inhabitants; that in the cotton manufacture, nearly half of the total value of products has similar classification; and that but

[1] Vol. VII, pp. cxc–ccxvii.

slightly more than one-third of the total value of iron
and steel products is reported from the cities where
the business is localized. These illustrations may suffice to show how erroneous is the impression that
great cities are absorbing the manufactures of the
whole country, and that mills and factories are disap-
pearing from the villages and small cities. It is by no
means certain that the trust will find concentration of
production as profitable as consolidation of administration. Indeed, it is conceivable that the highest economy would be realized in a common management of
plants advantageously located wherever the raw material and the labor supply and the market determine
the situation. It is not improbable that the small city
will retain a competitive chance, even if the trust continues ; but it should not be forgotten that many lines
of manufacture have escaped the trust altogether, and
that even in those industries in which consolidation has
been most prominent, a multitude of small establishments remain outside. Whatever the future may reveal, the signs now are that the small city and the
village are to be permanent factors in our industrial
civilization.

It is needless to speculate when the facts are spread
before us in the census itself. The investigation might
be made exhaustive and conclusive, but it is deemed
sufficient to examine the tables of population for Vermont, Massachusetts, New York, and Ohio, with a
view to ascertaining the growth or decline of villages
and small cities having from 2,500 to 8,000 inhabitants.
Accuracy is impossible, for a rural population is in-

cluded in the town totals for New England, and other cases are confusing. A general statement, accurate enough for our purpose, may be made, that Vermont may have a single case, and Massachusetts one or two cases of such villages losing population. It is not clear that Illinois affords an example of such loss, while New York contains ten or a dozen of these losing villages and small cities. It would seem that manufacturing sustains the Massachusetts villages, and that in Illinois they are prosperous trade centres and places of residence for retired farmers. Vermont, perhaps, shows a combination of agricultural and manufacturing support. Certainly it is remarkable that in villages of this size in these three states growth is so nearly universal. The case of New York tempts one to offer the conjecture that local manufactures lack the support which they receive from an environment like that of Massachusetts, and that the agricultural base is less thrifty than in Illinois. Or perhaps it is enough to say that New York happens to have towns whose growth from trade culminated in the period corresponding to the present time in Illinois, a much newer state, and whose manufactures have not expanded, as is the case with similar villages in Massachusetts. These sporadic examples of a slight decline in population are so extraordinary in the census tables that they provoke inquiry; the broad fact is that larger villages and small cities are growing. It would not be justifiable in every instance to infer thrift from a mere increase of population, for it is conceivable that a larger number of people might be less amply furnished with industrial opportunity, but there can be no serious error in the common interpretation of growth as indicating prosperity.

The thrifty village everywhere meets the eye of the traveller. The tendency towards agglomeration appears all the way down from the metropolis to the hamlet. Many small villages, of course, have fared badly in the changes wrought by railways and factories. The older sections are dotted with church spires in the midst of clusters of houses on remote hilltops or beside lonely highways. Decay in such hamlets as these usually is matched by growth in some new centre of population. The flourishing village is characteristic of the time. These pleasant and thriving centres, strewn through the rural districts, mark the zone of growth. Though not found everywhere, they are so common that every one knows them by scores, or if he be a traveller in wider circuits, by hundreds.[1]

This account of rural growth should not close without reference to a new development of great promise. Irrigation has played a great part in economic history, and it may be predicted with confidence that the finest rural civilization will be found ultimately on irrigated lands, where the density of population, the large rewards of labor, the combination of urban and rural advantages, favor the highest social development. With modern appliances at command, a new kind of exist-

---

[1] Cf. Twelfth Census, U. S., Vol. I, p. xc. The semi-urban population (towns and cities having 4,000–8,000 inhabitants) between 1890 and 1900 increased from 6,172,275 to 8,208,480. This increase appears in all the states except Wyoming and Nevada,—three states being omitted in this part of the table.

ence will be achieved, and multitudes will have again the opportunity of a Garden of Eden. If they escape moral disaster in the affluence of this material environment, they may lead the way to new social altitudes. The admirable Irrigation Law of 1902 inaugurated this phase of our national progress on a great scale, and at every point guarded the interests of the actual occupants of small areas.

The story of the country town is not wholly a tale of depletion. He who tells it thus obscures many facts, and what is more important, precisely those facts that mark the path of future developments. When after an epoch of subsidence, islands emerge from the sea, these first upheavals reveal the rising of sunken lands. The worst is now over. Prosperous farms and thriving villages throughout the zone of rural growth are an earnest of the good time to come when the whole countryside will flourish. Meanwhile the depleted tract occasions grave anxiety.

BOOK II

THE QUESTION OF CHARACTER

"The true records of mankind, the human annals of the earth, are not to be found in the changes of geographical names, in the shifting boundaries of dominion, in the travels and adventures of the baubles of royalty, or even in the undulations of the greater and lesser waves of population. We have learned nothing, till we have penetrated far beyond these casual and external changes, which are of interest only as the effect and symptoms of the great mental vicissitudes of our race. History is an account of the past experience of humanity; and this, like the life of the individual, consists in the ideas and sentiments, the deeds and passions, the truths and toils, the virtues and the guilt, of the mind and heart within."

—*James Martineau*, " *Endeavors after the Christian Life*," *p. 218.*

" For our historian, in numberless instances, offers us the mere surface and ragged edges of a happening, as though this were the whole of it. . . . It is only when we begin to realize that every event in addition to its outer form, has an inward life of its own, mystical, infinitely complex, whose full development may take centuries and millenniums to unfold, that we are in a position to study it aright."

—*J. Brierly*, " *Ourselves and the Universe*," *pp. 29, 30.*

CHAPTER V

LOCAL DEGENERACY

The foregoing chapters have discussed changes of great importance and interest, but their chief value for our purpose is in the foundation that they lay for the study of the ethical development of the country people. " The undulations of the greater and lesser waves of population "—to borrow a phrase that sums up our statistical investigations—must be construed to the imagination in their tragic meanings of personal success and misfortune, and interpreted in their bearing upon social progress and their influence upon the intellectual and moral character of individuals and communities. Were it a question of individual character only, much could be said of the power of environment over men. Whatever may be the superior man's power of resistance, " men of inferior degree " are moulded by external conditions. " Men such as these will not master, or alter within them, the event that they meet; nay, they themselves become morally transformed by the very first thing that draws near them." [1] In the case of communities, the transformation is accelerated as the waves of population ebb and flow, for the selection of some to go and of others to stay alters the social composition. To change the figure, as heat alters the molecular structure of iron

[1] Maurice Maeterlinck, " Wisdom and Destiny," p. 117.

95

so that the blow of the hammer easily shapes it, so the disintegration within the community makes it more plastic. And if the change of population goes so far as to put a strain upon social institutions, moral tenacity may suffer yet more seriously. We will not ask here concerning the forces at work for good or ill in the rural population; it may suffice to say that no reason appears for distrusting the powerful moral influence of such radical changes in the rural environment as have been set forth. The question of fact should be considered without the bias of speculation.

Nor should an appreciation of the interests at stake perturb the judgment; and yet the gravity of the inquiry should be felt, for only thus will the mind be disposed to proper caution and thoroughness. When we ask how the country people are acquitting themselves in their moral warfare, the question concerns the fortune of half mankind in our part of the world. By actual count of heads, the people of farm and village deserve equal consideration with the more conspicuous masses of the city. In our own country three in five of the people, be it remembered, still live in towns of less than 2,500 inhabitants;[1] and until there are great changes in the form of civilization, it will be necessary for a man to live somewhere in the country as the partner of the man who lives in the city. Insignificant as a single country town may be as compared with great cities, the aggregate rural population is vast and imposing.

The significance of the rural condition is enhanced

[1] Cf. p. 42.

—and for many this is the chief matter—by the moral contribution of the country to the city. The city is better equipped for independence than when Emerson wrote: " The city would have died out, rotted, and exploded, long ago, but that it was reinforced from the fields," [1] for in modern conditions the natural increase of its own people would keep it full and its own social forces would check decadence. Thus far, nevertheless, country-bred men have dominated our entire civilization, and therefore any suggestion that the country has become impoverished, and that the rural sources of intelligence and character are approaching exhaustion, excites grave apprehension.

Our inquiry has to do primarily with the depleted town. Were all country towns growing, it would occur to no one to ask whether they, in distinction from the rest of the world, are making moral progress. The pessimist and the optimist, doubtless, would wax earnest in the familiar debate concerning the character of modern civilization, and each would be able to find material for his argument in every part of the land. It is the thinning out of the rural population that has startled the observer and aroused the theorist. It is, of course, possible for a depleted town to make intellectual and moral gains. If farms were consolidated by the sale of unprofitable lands to the richest farmers, if the new owners introduced improved methods of cultivation, if social intercourse were skillfully adapted to the changed conditions, if the educational and ecclesiastical structure were remodelled, the

[1] "Essays," Second Series, Manners, Riverside Ed., Vol. III, p. 126.

population might be depleted to almost any extent without social or moral injury. At the best, however, such adjustment will be slowly wrought and many communities will fail of it altogether.

On the other hand, the growing town possesses no moral insurance. The increase of population may be due to some industry that supports an alien and inferior labor colony. In that case the decay of the native stock, the weakening of social institutions, and all the consequences of depletion may be the same as in towns that have not received this indigestible increment of population. The census is by no means an infallible guide to the area within which the changes under consideration are found.

When matters of fact are to be determined, the authority is the eye-witness, for the man who has seen with his own eyes is to be trusted rather than the man who has not seen, whatever may be the seeming wisdom of his speculations. If it were possible to summon competent witnesses from a sufficient number and variety of localities, their testimony would be final, and social theorizing would be restricted by these determining observations. It is fair to say, however, that the most honest eye-witness cannot free himself wholly from personal bias, for some facts appeal to him and others escape his notice as certainly as he possesses a distinctive inclination and interest. The picture that he paints represents his selection, grouping, and interpretation of the items actually before his eyes. If he is of a pessimistic temper, or if he is an artist delighting in sombre effects, his handling of light and shade

will not present the moral landscape exactly as it is.
In point of fact almost all of those who feel the
artistic interest in an impression, do deepen the
shadows by emphasizing the remnant of a larger
population, the decay of schools where once were
crowds of children, the abandonment of farms, the
forsaking of churches,—changes incident to modern
progress. The literary artist has full right to these
shadows; all that is pointed out is that he is likely to
avail himself of them in such a manner that his canvas
will have a look unlike a more scientific presentation
of the same conditions.   And to this it must be added
that in serious discussion there is no equivalent for the
literary appeal to the imagination and the feeling, as
the tragedy of some broken life is set forth, or the
quaint backwardness of a decadent region is portrayed.
The artist has the great human interests on his side,
and summaries and generalizations, however carefully
and wisely framed, are ineffective in comparison.

An example may make the matter plain. Some
years ago a correspondent of the New York *Evening
Post* wrote at length and with much telling detail
concerning the New England churches. The article
appeared with the following headlines: " Decay of
Religion in Rural Communities—A Mournful Review
—Changes of Twenty Years—Pitiful State of a Christian Minister—The Root of the Trouble." Here we
have the deepening of the shadow by the artful use
of social change, and the vivid portrayal of local conditions, and the appeal to sympathy by a pathetic
personal example. The account of " church buildings

crumbling and old church societies dead"; of "family after family and hamlet after hamlet that have not seen a church service in years"; of "communities that might as well have been in the middle of the Dark Continent so far as Christianizing influences are concerned"; of the "social chaos" about these "deserted houses of worship"—was so graphic and so startling that it remained in my memory, although a masterly reply filed with it was forgotten. So alarming was this representation that a citizen of New York, who knew New England well, was stirred up to make an investigation. He sent out two hundred letters to the most intelligent men whose names were obtainable in each of the New England states, asking for an opinion based upon their observation of actual conditions. About one hundred and fifty replies were received, and their comments on the situation were a complete exposure of the false impression produced by an adroit use of selected facts. In the main it was found that conditions had not been misrepresented in their actual local character, although the personal touch was gained by repeating the story of an insane minister as told by himself. The items in this debate need not concern us; reference is made to it only to show how much less impressive is general prosperity than local decadence. It would not be possible to tell the story of religious life as it goes forward in hundreds of churches in a way to arrest attention or charge the memory. There is no news value—perhaps no literary or artistic value—in the wholesome averages of life.

With such precautions as have been suggested, there is no reason to discredit the tales of rural decadence told by eye-witnesses. Certainly the existence of an abandoned meeting-house is a fact to be accepted, if a truthful observer has seen it. The same may be said of " twenty-five wretched families of the degenerate type in a single town," and of a " family in which grandparents, adult children, and grandchildren are all foolish." Degenerate families by the score, and families with three generations of idiots are easily observed, labeled, and certified. It is idle to ask whether degenerate families or three generations of idiots can be matched in the city; it is sufficiently shocking that they are found in the country. Reasoning from such facts is precarious, but facts once correctly observed must take their place in social estimates. What then are the facts observed in country towns,—exceptional perhaps and less significant than might be supposed, but unquestionable facts that must be taken into account?

The New York *Evening Post*, commenting on the article to which reference was made above, said: " Rural life is monotonous and hard, with nothing in it to stimulate the imagination or refine the taste. The closest observers will soonest admit that by consequence the grosser forms of vice and crime in rural communities abound more than in great cities with all the slums counted in." Although the comparison with cities is not sustained by statistics,[1] this arraignment of rural communities for grosser forms of vice

[1] Cf. p. 113.

and crime has much local justification. In its issue of January 2, 1904, the St. Albans (Vt.) *Messenger* quoted from the Montpelier *Argus:* " The two recent murder trials in Bennington County and the one now in progress in Windsor County reveal a surprising state of depravity, a condition of affairs that might be expected to lead to murder in any community. Lack of education, lack of moral training, and lack of uplifting environment, as much as lack of individual character and stamina, account for the crimes. Such conditions are not usual in Vermont, but they appear here as elsewhere, and bring the usual and expected results." The following editorial comment was added, with more to the same effect : " And the *Messenger* contends that it is not vilifying the state, it is not proclaiming her degenerate, for public spirited newspapers to point out this fact to their readers and to emphasize it so often and so vigorously that the popular mind will be induced to pay that heed to it that it deserves."

An editorial in the *Boston Herald* of March 9, 1903, places two prosperous New England states side by side in this deplorable local degeneracy. It says in part: " A few years ago a writer in the *Atlantic Monthly* gave a picture of the deterioration of the quality of character and life in the remote hill towns of Massachusetts. His statements were received with incredulity, and were sharply contradicted by others who thought they knew better than he did the real conditions in such communities. One would suppose that what was said less than two weeks ago about the degeneracy of rural Connecticut in an address in New

Haven before the Connecticut Bible Society, by the Rev. H. L. Hutchins, was new and strange, judging by the attention it has received. This attention is possibly more keen than it would have been if the teacher had not since died suddenly, making the deliverance seem like a prophet's last word of instruction and warning. It was a very solemn and important message, the substantial truth of which is accepted by the Connecticut newspapers with a unanimity that would hardly have been thought probable. He tells a story of degeneracy and immorality which is rather worse than the story told by the writer of the articles in the *Atlantic Monthly*, to which we have referred. Yet no one is assailing it as a misstatement, and Massachusetts newspapers, in commenting on it, take pains to say that we have no cause to congratulate ourselves on the existence of better conditions here. We observe no such swift disposition to contradict the truth of the dreadful message as was manifest formerly. Does this mean that in the interval a conviction has spread that the wickedness of some of our rural neighborhoods is not exaggerated by those who have probed them to find the truth? The address of Mr. Hutchins was supplemented by an article which he wrote on the day of his unexpected death. The two constitute a body of testimony which neither the social nor the religious world can safely ignore."

The articles in the *Atlantic Monthly* [1] were written with high color, being in the best style of the literary

---

[1] Rollin Lynde Hartt, "A New England Hill Town," *Atlantic Monthly*, Vol. LXXXIII.

impressionist. The decadence described was easily recognized as characteristic of other places, if not of " Sweet Auburn." Nothing criminal was alleged, but rather incompetence, dullness, decay lapsing into idiocy. The narrowness of the horizon, the pettiness of the endless gossip, the absence of ambition, the feebleness of faculties as if the string had broken and the bundle fallen apart, were graphically presented and evidently drawn from life.

The testimony of Mr. Hutchins has every title to respect : it was based upon the observation of many years during which it had been his business to go from house to house upon an errand that made him watchful of moral conditions ; more important still, in its utterance there is a note of sharp pain, as if a constantly confronted horror had burned his soul. His story dwells upon the prevalent ignorance, the inroads of vice, the open contempt of marriage, the increase of idiocy, the feebleness and backwardness of schools, the neglect of the church, the swift lapse into virtual heathenism in whole sections once occupied by the best type of Christian manhood.[1] The last phrase is not stronger than one used by President William D. Hyde, who, writing of religious conditions in Maine, launched a magazine article under the title, " Impending Paganism in New England."[2]

The chapter in " The New Era " in which Dr. Strong treats the problem of the country is deeply

---

[1] Such local reports as these do not mean that the country churches of Connecticut as a whole are not vigorous and successful in their work.

[2] *The Forum*, June, 1892.

shadowed.[1] The melancholy results of depletion, with the emphasis upon the neglect of religion, are vividly portrayed. Then comes the summary under five heads : Road deteriorate; property depreciates; churches and schools are impaired; the foreign crowds out the native stock; isolation increases with a tendency towards degeneration and demoralization. The conclusion is stated in the terms of momentum and velocity that distinguish the writings of this modern prophet, to whom nothing is stationary but all things in swift rush towards destiny. " If this migration continues," he says, " and no new preventive measures are devised, I see no reason why isolation, irreligion, ignorance, vice, and degradation should not increase in the country until we have a rural American peasantry, illiterate and immoral, possessing the rights of citizenship, but utterly incapable of performing or comprehending its duties." Doubtless Dr. Strong has hope that " preventive measures " will be devised, but he leaves us with the thrill of that frightful slide towards bottomless misery upon us. That should stir us to seek " preventive measures," for it is impossible to deny this moral gravitation. There is in full action such a tendency as this towards degradation; in the main it may be counteracted—it is possible that Providence has set in operation " preventive measures " of high efficiency. What we are here to recognize is the inevitable movement towards decadence,—a movement everywhere felt, and where not resisted, producing that visible degeneracy described by so many witnesses.

[1] See particularly pp. 170-174.

Rural life is everywhere on an inclined plane; if it climbs instead of slides, great should be our thankfulness. Beyond question, in some places it slides.

We have no call to deny such alleged facts as have been presented in the preceding paragraphs. It is not our purpose, on the other hand to establish them, since so much of this sort has been written that it is quite unnecessary to cover the ground again. Enough has been presented to enable the reader to conceive this aspect of the rural situation. We shall not credit every gruesome tale; we shall allow something for panic, and something for art, and something for the intense realization of the reformer. The residuum of truth finds its place in that general conception of a world-wide revolution in rural life which is a vital part of modern progress. It is a thing to be expected that where the change has been made with least success, where the strain has been greatest, serious decadence should appear. Indeed it is no exaggeration to say that tendencies are at work which unchecked would ruin all rural communities. The inclined plane on which every country town must secure its footing is no fiction; towns that slip may slide far.

CHAPTER VI

THE MAIN TREND

In his essay, " The Mission of Humor," the best of whose delightful surprisés are odd glimpses of truth, Dr. Crothers points out a most interesting characteristic of the " prosaic theorist." " He tries to get all the facts under one formula," which is a very " ticklish business," being indeed " like the game of pigs in clover." " He gets all the facts but one into the inner circle. By a dexterous thrust he gets that one in, and the rest are out." By dint of great persistence and cunning the theorist sometimes gets all rural communities into clover, but that ends the game. Usually there is no such success, for as the recalcitrant specimen is thrust in, a scampering company breaks out with much noise and raising of dust. He who would maintain that all country towns are prosperous, or that all are decadent, will find the crowd of irrepressible facts too much for his dexterity and vigilance. Nevertheless the seduction of a general formula is not easily resisted,—like a modern navy, once possessed it must be used. Charles Lamb is held up by Dr. Crothers as a wholesome model of a philosopher who saves himself no end of trouble by leaving the last pig out. " He does not try to fit all the facts to one theory. That seems to him too economical, when theories are so cheap. With large-hearted generosity he provides a theory for every fact. He clothes the ragged exception with all the decent habiliments of a universal law. He picks up a little ragamuffin of a fact, and warms its heart and points out its great relations." [1]

We are willing to be as generous as Charles Lamb; we will provide a special theory for the decadent country town. Have we not sought to " clothe this ragged exception with all the decent habiliments of a universal law "? What more can be asked than that we recognize local degeneracy, equip it with an explanation, and give it the standing of an inevitable fact under modern conditions? But when we have done this, it is enough. We refuse to introduce all facts into the same society. We are willing to take this little vagabond of a fact, make the most of him, warm his heart, tell the tale of great relations; but when all is done, we brand him a ragamuffin, although a very interesting one, and shut the door of good society in his face. Why should all pigs be in clover, except in a game? And why should every uncouth fact be permitted to cherish the dream of universal equality? The humorist finds in exceptions and odd remainders—things left over in the cosmic workshop—abundant materials for his art. The decadent town is such an intractable remainder in the evolution of civilization,—more pathetic than humorous, but above all things calling for the sympathetic treatment that recognizes the unique exception.

We proceed, therefore, to arrange rural facts in two

[1] Samuel McChord Crothers, " The Gentle Reader," pp. 84, 85.

systems, the system of decadence and the system of progress. Some communities are in the main trend of prosperity; others are off the track of the modern movement in various stages of deterioration or mere backwardness. It is obvious that descriptions of one social condition will not apply to the other. It has been customary, nevertheless, to treat all rural facts in one class, especially in statistical summaries. If it is remembered that communities are either adjusted or not adjusted to modern conditions, that they are in or out of the trend of progress, that they are decadent or prosperous, it will appear of how little use the ordinary general formula is. The average is an abstraction, useful for comparison but rarely available as an account of fact as it is in itself. The average elevation of the earth's surface would be interesting to know; but land, being solid and not flowing to a level like the sea, towers in mountain and sinks in valley, so that scarcely a square mile is spread out at the average altitude. Thus uneven is human society, with elevation matching depression, and few communities poised midway on the scale.

From general summaries the main trend of prosperity may be deduced convincingly, and no better way to make sure of it is available. We know that there is decadence. Prior to observation one may be certain that some towns are worse than others. If the average is known and the inferior proved, the existence of the superior is established. Let us see what comes of this method. In the social and moral diagnosis of the country town, much has been made of such symp-

toms as crime, insanity, idiocy, divorce, fecundity,
health, and longevity. It would detain us too long to
cite statistics in all these matters, and to discuss them
in detail. And this is as needless as it would be weari-
some, for it has been done by others with thoroughness
and discrimination. Weber has done excellent work
in comparing city and country in these particulars, and
we may safely rest our argument upon his results. In
any case our contention is not affected by a slight
movement of the rural average above or below the
urban average. This careful investigator finds that
crime,[1] insanity,[2] and divorce[3] are more abundant in
the city; that idiocy is more prevalent in the country; that marriage and fecundity[4] depend upon ideals
of life and social standards, and are but slightly influenced by rural or urban conditions; that the country
formerly had the advantage in health and length of
life,[5] but at present finds a strong competitor in the
city favored by modern sanitation. If all these points
of comparison are taken together, the result is distinctly favorable to the country. It is probable that in
towns which we class as decadent, all these symptoms
of social disease are aggravated; that in such towns
there would be more crime, more insanity and idiocy,

[1] " The Growth of Cities," pp. 403–409.   [2] *Ibid.*, pp. 392, 393.
[3] *Ibid.*, pp. 329, 330. Cf. Francis G. Peabody, " Jesus Christ and
the Social Question," p. 164.
[4] *Ibid.*, pp. 318–343, 367. Cf. Arthur Twining Hadley, " Economics," pp. 48, 49. Also Walter Bagehot, " Physics and Politics,"
pp. 195–200.
[5] *Ibid.*, pp. 343–367.

more divorce, more physical unsoundness than in the
city; that the familiar tales of rural degeneracy exceed
in frightfulness anything that is characteristic of the
cities as a whole.   Whether the decadent towns are
worse than the slums of cities, it is impossible to say,
for there are no statistics for such limited areas, and
personal impressions can have no authority.   But such
comparisons between grades of evil are of slight significance, inasmuch as there is every occasion for
alarm and every incentive to effort in the dark sections
of both city and country.   Our argument rests upon
the favorable showing of the country as a whole as
compared with the city as a whole.   As tested by the
symptoms of degeneracy, the country is in as healthful
a state as the city, where the advantages and wholesome influences of civilization are massed; where education is at its best; where eloquence finds its opportunity and art gathers its treasures; where wealth
commands all resources and taste has every gratifica-
tion; where churches are powerful and every social
institution coöperates in the exaltation of human life.
That the country is not distanced by the city in social
and moral development almost exceeds belief, or to
use the terms with which we began, the line of averages
in social and moral values is at a surprising height in
the country.   Now if a part of the rural communities
fall below this line, then other communities rise above
it; assuredly as many are above as below the line, or
it is falsely called an average.   These rural communities rising to these moral heights, constituting these
uplands of purity and health, determine and reveal the

configuration of the social landscape; their elevation marks the main trend.

Idiocy, to take the clearest case, is more common in the country than in the city. It does not follow that all rural life is under a mental blight. One easily goes astray in speaking of this deplorable misfortune, for when all is said, highly intellectual parents are not infrequently afflicted with feeble-minded children. There seems to be an element of accident or mischance in their birth, and it is not irrational to suppose that the more delicate and elaborate combinations of the elements that transmit personality most easily suffer disaster. It is probable, also, that the city isolates the feeble-minded, prevents their marriage, educates them, if capable of education, more generally than is the case in the country. One would not look for three generations of idiots in the city; that should be possible only in some retired spot where the individual escapes the espionage of society. These remarks go far to arrest the suspicion that something in the nature of rural life tends to the increase of idiocy. At the utmost it is not conspicuous anywhere. If the point is still pressed that idiocy is found in the country in an alarming degree, it is fair to say that any excess beyond what is due to accident, which cannot be foreseen nor controlled, and to direct inheritance, which always bespeaks social negligence, may be assigned with reasonable confidence to the decadent communities. It is not strange that a degenerate stock in a decadent society produces an abnormal number of feeble-minded children. One may boldly challenge the production of proof that the better country towns give any sign of increasing or alarming idiocy.

Statistics of crime yield a result favorable to the country ; and yet as in the case of idiocy it is possible that if decadent towns could be considered by themselves, among their bums and hoodlums and degenerates, crimes—especially crimes of violence and crimes against morals—would be more numerous than in cities,—more numerous, it might be, than in the slums of cities, as the New York *Evening Post* charged. That scathing arraignment of rural life, quoted in the preceding chapter, did not discriminate, however, between communities which were evidently in the mind of the writer and all communities. The distinction is of great importance, for certainly towns which have never seen a crime within their borders ought not to be characterized in the same terms as towns in which repeated crimes bring to light conditions that induce outbreaks against the moral order. The criminal, of course, may appear anywhere without warning, and his crime may be no consequence of local corruption. He may be a passing visitor, a tramp from other environments, an immigrant for whom the community is not responsible ; or he may be an unaccountable sport from the best human stock, bred for better things but bent in some deep fibre of the nature towards moral irregularity. Sporadic and without social significance as occasional crime may be, it would be the sheerest folly to ignore the causal connection between the decadence of communities and criminal tendencies. What may be said truthfully of crime in country towns should be restricted to those communities whose conditions develop it. It is as unjust to characterize all country towns as breeding places of crime as to charge upon all wards of cities the vices of their slums.

The discrimination upon which we insist is clearly apprehended and stated by Professor Giddings. " Degeneration," he says, " manifests itself in the protean forms of suicide, insanity, crime, and vice, which abound in the highest civilization, where the tension of life is extreme, and in those places from which civilization has ebbed and from which population has been drained, leaving a discouraged remnant to struggle against deteriorating conditions. . . . Like insanity, crime occurs most frequently in densely populated towns on the one hand, and on the other in partially deserted rural districts. Murder is a phenomenon of both the frontier life of an advancing population and of the declining civilization in its rear ; it is preeminently the crime of the new town and the decaying town. . . . Crimes of all kinds are less frequent in prosperous agricultural communities and in thriving towns of moderate size, where the relation of income to the standard of living is such that the life struggle is not severe."

The view of this writer concerning " the high rate of insanity in lonely farming districts " has much pertinency, although it should not be forgotten that the collapse of the brain is the proper consequence of the intensity and difficulty of a feverish city life. " The isolated farmer and his family," it is pointed out, " have begun to be affected by the strain of modern life in a deplorable way. They are no longer ignorant of the luxuries of the towns and a simple manner of life no longer satisfies them. The house must be remodelled and refurnished ; the table must be varied ; clothing must be ' in style ' and the horses, carriages, and harnesses must be more costly. The impossibility of maintaining this scale of expense under existing agricultural conditions embitters life, and finally, in many cases, destroys the mental balance." [1] This, doubtless, is that grain of truth to be found in the oft-repeated assertion that the farmhouse is productive of insanity, particularly in the case of women. It is, of course, a condition, rather than a location, that fosters insanity, and this condition is met most frequently in the depleted town that has sunk into decadence. Yet not the sunken but the sinking town is most likely to develop insanity, and possibly crime also. There must be the vision of unattainable things and the desperate mood of disappointment to drive the mind to madness ; in stagnancy contentment and peace are not difficult.

With the exception of idiocy, every kind of human defect that the census tabulates, which sociologists emphasize in discussing degeneracy, is more rare in the country than in the city. This is the case in spite of appalling increments of these disorders in a portion of the rural communities. What, then, must be the vital and spiritual health of that rural wholesomeness that so decisively turns the balance ! There must be vast tracts of prosperous and happy rural life, wide

[1] Franklin Henry Giddings, " The Principles of Sociology," pp. 348, 349.

regions in which the adjustment to new conditions has been made. The dismal facts on the one side are more than outnumbered by cheering facts on the other side.

The outcome from this point of view, first of all, is fear, as we see the wreck of communities at the bottom of the decline. The impression under which the preceding chapter closed is still upon us. A process that issues in these melancholy results wherever it is unchecked, is in full movement throughout the area of modern civilization. Like individuals, communities have life and death set before them, and some choose death,—for it is never thrust upon the unconsenting; others choose life,—for it is not won without resolution.

From this discrimination of the double issue comes, also, the appeal to courage. The times are caught in the drift of evolution in such powerful grip that if men will, they are borne onward to desired success. It behooves strenuous men to make friends with the reigning powers. By studying the times, by catching step with the movement of the age, by winning adaptation to the new environment, rural communities may make the great transition from the outworn to the coming civilization with safety and high hope. Always with more or less of intelligence, with more or less of moral heroism, there is a vast adjustment to the demand of evolution. Silently, as when the temple was built without sound of hammer, the new civilization develops.

What we have denominated the main trend, is that vigorous and prosperous rural life which has passed the crisis of the times successfully. With slight exceptions, the zone of rural growth which was traced in an earlier chapter, is included in the sweep of this hopeful and inspiring development, but many depleted towns are ranged in this domain of courage and discriminating optimism. There is no fatality in the loss of population; the prunning of a people may yield a good return in thrift and virtue. So much is clear; but how to measure the effects of emigration upon the quality of a remnant, and how to conceive the demand for an altered social structure, require a study of evolutionary forces and of social reconstruction wholly different in scope and method from the statistical inquiries and the observation of conditions in which we have been engaged.

BOOK III

THE INCIDENCE OF SELECTION

" The law of natural selection and the conception of life as a process of adjustment of the organism to its environment have become the core of the biology and the psychology of to-day. It was inevitable that the evolutionary philosophy should be extended to embrace the social phenomena of human life. The science that had traced life from protoplasm to man could not stop with explanations of his internal constitution. It must take cognizance of his manifold external relations, of the ethical groups, of the natural societies of men, and of all the phenomena that they exhibit, and inquire whether these things also are not products of the universal evolution."

—*Franklin Henry Giddings, "The Principles of Sociology," p. 7.*

CHAPTER VII

THE HERITAGE OF UNFITNESS

As set forth in the preceding pages, the key to the main problems of country life is the thinning out of the rural population in consequence of industrial changes. Our discussion has dealt with the causes, the extent, and the probable continuance of this depletion. To this there has been added a brief survey of the more obvious moral results—degeneracy in the more isolated and backward regions, and ethical soundness where the adjustment to the new social order has been made. We might pass at once to the social problems upon which we seek light, but in that case we should miss the most interesting phases of the subject. We should be like the explorer who follows the Niagara through the wild and fascinating Rapids and turns aside for a shorter route to the lower lake before beholding the Falls in which the mighty forces of the river are revealed. In the rural population is a most interesting exhibition of evolutionary forces. It is beyond question that man is under that system of development through birth and death, through heredity and environment, which has filled sea and land with the countless species of living things; and this process of evolution appears in the changes we have noted. What is taking place can be understood fully only by tracing this operation of the forces that alter the forms of life as science now conceives it. A practical discussion permits only such a survey as suggests how rich the field is for the evolutionist who will cultivate it in the interest of science. All that we venture is to take glimpses of this man-making as it goes forward in country towns.

To many evolution as applied to man suggests only the perplexing problem of his origin; far more important is the fact that the moment man appears he finds himself under the laws that are regnant in the transformation of living creatures. Natural selection, certainly, operates upon the human species as effectively as upon any order of life. Indeed, man is transformed under new pressures of environment more rapidly and more completely than any other creature. On the one hand, his natural feebleness and sensitiveness hasten the sifting of death, and, on the other hand, his vast diversity in mental and social and spiritual powers offers an unparalleled range to selection. The ascent to humanity, doubtless, was along the path thus marked out, and the method of progress is fixed by these conditions.

The country town, once containing too many people and now depleted, presents a unique field for natural selection. Much depends upon the elements of the population lost and retained. If the best have gone, the type of man must degenerate; if the worst have dropped out, the average man must improve as the generations work out results,—unless other influences afford compensation. Our first task, as we turn to the principles of evolution, is to trace the incidence of selection.

The typical evolutionary process consists in the production of an excess of individuals—of eleven, for example, where ten can live, as has been the case with the country people during recent decades—and in the destruction of those least suited to the environment. This repeated again and again tends to change the species. The essential thing is the production of unfit individuals to be crowded out, without which nature would be tied up—gripped in the fatal equilibrium of balanced forces. That condition of overpopulation which has entailed much hardship is full of promise for evolution. Those least adapted to the rural environment have gone from the country towns—so much is certain, but always the issue is in doubt until one knows whether the worst or the best are eliminated. The best, as measured by universal standards, may be the unadapted, in which case there will be degeneracy; or the worst may prove to be the unfit in the competition, in which case there will be progress. The probability is that the thinning of the rural population will rid the towns having large numbers of inferior persons of a considerable part of them. If this should happen, the benefit would be great. Before we can determine whether it happens or not, we must have a clear conception of the lowest stratum of the rural population. To this inquiry we must now address ourselves.

The view here maintained is that the country towns have had an excess of inferior stock, and that this condition dates from their beginning. If this is true, heritage is the correct term for much of the evil that now curses rural communities. Incidentally we gain the answer to many charges of degeneracy, for the badness that succeeds to badness is not deterioration. Our purpose is to find what human material is most likely to be selected for elimination in country towns, but we can afford to be thorough in the investigation because of its contribution to the belief that the present is not worse than the past. In general, worthless or inferior people in the country are descendants of or successors to worthless and inferior people of former times. To this there are two notable exceptions, and these may be pointed out at the start.

Unquestionably there is a considerable degeneracy from a superior ancestry. A tendency to vital impairment and moral reaction is evident, as if human nature were an elastic bow that recovers a comfortable slackness after the flight of the arrow. In the case of the Puritan stock, which was overloaded with religious intensity and moral strenuousness, the penalty of a straining excellence is particularly clear, for the weaker constitutions, fevered by fanaticism, transmitted the vital injury to disordered generations in which crankiness, oddity, and freakishness run in the blood. A rare blend may yield the genius, but the odd genius turns up more frequently. Faddists are more numerous in the social centres,—queer characters in remote solitudes. Though this nervous and temperamental disturbance is a vast enrichment of humor, in any practical appraisal it must be deemed a lapse. The quaint and spicy variety of life, rarely found in the midst of sturdy progress, is the natural efflorescence of decay. Genius itself is hazardous ; often its possessors have a precarious existence and are short-lived. Much here depends upon the point of view. Unfitness for the tasks of present civilization suggests the gentleman of the old school, the poet, the visionary. We remember Plato's philosopher retiring under the shelter of a wall in the storm of dust and heat, content if only he can live his own life, keep himself pure from evil, and depart in peace and good will with bright hopes.[1] To such as these we affix no dishonoring name, but as we descend the scale of worth towards the illassorted débris of a great race, there is found an unfitness that is rightly termed degeneracy.

The other exception to the principle that unfitness is bred from unfitness has very great importance. The environment is changed radically for all country people, some of whom cannot adapt themselves to the new demands. There may be some lack of plasticity, some strange incapacity for catching the new pace, some excess of the conservative temper, in consequence of which superior people, as measured by the requirements of a former age, are wholly unsuited to the new time. Many men and women who adorn the past would be helpless incapables in the conditions of to-day; some that were saints in their time would not now be able to keep out of jail; things that once belonged to reputable life would not be tolerated in modern society. Much more apparent is industrial

[1] " The Republic," Book VI, p. 496.

incompetence when the skill of one age survives unchanged in a different time. No possible mastery of the hand loom can be anything but unfitness in an age of machinery. So far as the handicrafts have art values they merit cultivation, but the undiscriminating restoration of discarded household industries, in which some fantastic reformers have sought the way to the rural millennium, is a mistaken fostering of industrial incompetence.[1] Most disheartening is the unteachable conservatism that continues the use of ancient methods in times to which they are unsuited. Many a farmer is classed as decadent, who is every whit the equal of illustrious ancestors in the management of the farm. Just as the species formed for the sea could not thrive in the unsupporting and tenuous air until profoundly modified in every part of the skeleton and in every vital organ, so the farmer and the villager, moulded by the age of homespun, are unsuited to these new times without radical change.

How much of the unfitness now discoverable in country towns is derived from a past fitness in these two ways, it is impossible to say. To unfitness descending by direct heredity from unfitness, we will give more detailed attention.

The country town lends itself with peculiar facility to the idealizing mood in retrospect. Dream-touched memory fills the nearer years with fond illusion, and tradition inevitably glorifies remoter times. If we will

[1] For an interesting account of "The Revival of Fireside Industries" see an article in the *New England Magazine*, for December, 1903, by Katherine Louise Smith.

place our base line in this shadowy region, it will be necessary to make careful local discriminations. The past is of three kinds: there is the commercial sphere, comprising communities within fifty miles of tide water; there is an expanding and retreating frontier; and there is the area of homespun. No small part of the glory of the colonial period belongs to the sphere of commerce; as such it is urban rather than rural, although the centres of this traffic were but villages. In every period of our history the character of the frontiersman has commanded admiration,[1] but it is an idle task to consider whether a community deteriorates as the rugged virtues of the early settlers fail to be reproduced. The idyll of homespun, sung in the stately prose of Bushnell,—voicing as it does the common regard for the past,—confronts us as we enter the region affording typical conditions of age and situation. To find the facts in this land of enchantment is not easy, and one naturally shrinks from inquiring too closely into conditions covered by this glamour and charm.

It would be unfair to cite the testimony of witnesses who lived in this golden age—much more unjustifiable to accept the denunciations and rebukes of preachers; for always a vivid sense of existing evils and a happy ease in forgetting the defects of other times make men unsafe interpreters of their own age. "To-day is a king in disguise," says Emerson. "To-day always looks mean to the thoughtless, in the face of an

---

[1] But the frontier draws the "most shiftless and vicious," also, see "The Winning of the West," by Theodore Roosevelt, pp. 130, 131.

uniform experience that all good and happy actions are made up precisely of these blank to-days."[1] The thoughtful are but little wiser, and it would be easy to fill pages from old sermons to show how men felt in the midst of the times we now glorify; but perhaps nothing would be gained beyond confirming Lowell's caution:

> "Now ain't jes' the minute
> Thet ever fits us easy while we're in it."[2]

A sample or two, however, of the utterances which our predecessors were accustomed to hear from the pulpit may show how little encouragement they had to idealize themselves. Dr. Emmons has left in print a large number of sermons in which he reviewed the changes of his time,—the note of honest alarm is too evident to permit their being brushed aside as exaggerations due to homiletic fervor. As early as 1790 he said that religious assemblies are visibly diminishing; that family devotion and parental instruction and discipline are very generally neglected and despised; that many of the rising families neither exhibit the forms of religion, nor the examples of virtue; that these prayerless and irreligious homes are the hives of vice; that multitudes may be seen every day, and almost everywhere, wallowing in drunkenness, and glorying in their shame.[3] In 1821 this man, who is popularly supposed to have preached to a congrega-

---

[1] Lecture on the Times, Riverside Ed., Vol. I, p. 255.
[2] Biglow Papers, Riverside Ed., Vol. VIII, p. 335.
[3] The Works of Nathanael Emmons, D.D., Vol. V, pp. 33, 34.

tion in which all the people were gathered, used this language: "If the great majority agree to disregard the Sabbath as holy time, or neglect family worship as an uncommanded duty, or neglect attending public worship, half or all the day, or disbelieve the Bible, or deny its essential doctrines, or neglect family government, or allow and practice vain and sinful and demoralizing amusements, or despise and oppose the virtuous habits of their fathers, the minority inwardly approve and gradually follow the current of corruption. Is not this visible all over New England, and even among ourselves? Is there a fashionable evil among the multitude that the minority do not more or less approve, patronize and practice? Is it strange that moral declension is so little perceived, lamented, and restrained?" [1] These utterances and many more denouncing prevalent irreligion, profanity, gaming, prodigality, licentiousness, intemperance, cover the whole period in which the age of homespun was at its best.

Our great idealist has pointed out the reconciliation of these diverse estimates of the past. "He is ill-informed," said Emerson in his Historical Address at Concord, "who expects, on running down the town records for two hundred years, to find a church of saints, a metropolis of patriots, enacting wholesome and creditable laws. . . . In these assemblies, the public weal, the call of interest, duty, religion, were heard; and every local feeling, every private grudge, every suggestion of petulance and ignorance, were not

[1] The Works of Nathanael Emmons, D.D., Vol. V, p. 341.

less faithfully produced." His conclusion, "If the results of our history are approved as wise and good, it was yet a free strife; if the good counsel prevailed, the sneaking counsel did not fail to be suggested; freedom and virtue, if they triumphed, triumphed in a fair field," [1] is a true historical insight. A common habit is to conceive the past in the light of triumphant causes without recognition of defeated forces. This is to rob history of all nobility, for victory over a trivial opposition is not worthy of the name. That two sorts of men make history, another of our great literary prophets knew well, for the Commemoration Ode, that consecrates to deathless fame men

"Limbed like the old heroic breeds," [2]

crowned years of tireless invective and raillery, whose one aim was to arouse the inert multitude who thought that principles

"Ough' to be easy'z an ole pair o' shoes." [3]

The author of the Biglow Papers never could have been beguiled into indiscriminate praise of the epoch through which he lived. Neither the nearer nor the remoter past is pictured rightly as a placid equality of goodness.

In all the colonies there were men of the Puritan quality. Of many races and of many faiths, they felt

---

[1] "Miscellanies," pp. 50–52, Riverside Ed., Vol. XI.
[2] Riverside Ed., Vol. X, p. 22.
[3] *Ibid.*, Vol. VIII, p. 324.

that spell of idealism under which the opening of a new
world everywhere bore the mark of a search for
Utopia. They abound in Pennsylvania and Ohio and
New York—in parts of the West and the South also
—as in New England. These are the real founders of
the nation; with them came people of another sort.
It is well known that Virginia, which was settled in
the main by excellent families, received a large immigration of an inferior character. The demand of the
tobacco plantations for labor caused the ships that
penetrated the whole tide-water region to bring over
loads of wretched men and women from the slums and
jails of the English seaports. In Virginia the commercial zone extended to the frontier, and nothing in her
development answers to the homespun civilization; but
her experience disproves the assertion that none but
high-minded and able men braved the perils of the
long voyage and the hardships of the wilderness in
those days,—and this lesson from her settlement is
available for our argument. Mr. John Fiske, with
evident reluctance, admits that, though not many such
worthless people came to New England, traces of the
" mean white " are found there; that isolated groups
" show strong points of resemblance to that ' white
trash ' which has come to be a recognizable strain of
the English race "; and that such riffraff may now and
then have crept in in spite of the effort of the New England colonies to keep it out. He approves the sentiment
of the election sermon of 1688: " God sifted a whole
nation, that he might send choice grain into the wilderness," and he stoutly maintains that " in all history

there has been no other instance of colonization so exclusively effected by picked and chosen men." [1]   Nothing but actually coming upon " Hardscrabble " or
" Hellhuddle " could have extorted this concession
from him, for in an earlier work he had written :
" The lowest ranks were not represented in the emigration ; and all idle, shiftless, or disorderly people
were rigorously refused admission into the new communities. . . . To an extent unparalleled, therefore, in the annals of colonization, the settlers of New
England were a body of picked men." [2]

With all deference for the authority of a favorite
historian, who would have written many far duller
pages if he had not dealt honestly with the seamy side
of history, it is submitted that any conceivable screen-
ing of the early immigration must have let pass more
riffraff than this ideal settlement supposes. [3]   The
better the stock, the more numerous will be the servants and dependents.   And what is quite as much to
the point, the finest families fray out in spots, so that
while one brother maintains the family dignity, another
finds his level in the group of village drunkards that
few communities fail to develop.   Nor should it be forgotten that in the settlement of the colonies there was
much that was not akin to the Puritan idealism.   There
were money-making enterprises in those days, and astute
promoters beguiled many unfortunates into the wilderness.   Hordes of the discontented sought to mend

[1] " The beginnings of New England," pp. 154, 155.   Illustrated Ed.
[2] " American Political Ideas," p. 29.
[3] Cf. Barrett Wendell, " A Literary History of America," p. 236.

their fortunes in the new world; multitudes thought more of fish and lumber, of a home and a farm, than of political or religious ideals. The adventurous and the restless felt the charm of a wild life. The saints, we may be sure, had no monopoly of either ships or charters.

The emphasis of history has fallen upon the like-mindedness of the older communities, formed under the Puritan impulse, which carried into the wilderness a complete social outfit. The church, the school, the town-meeting—not to mention distinctly socialistic arrangements—expressed and perpetuated a unique fellowship in the earliest settlements. The great majority of towns, however, had no such happy experience,—slowly evolving, as they did, from the scattered homes of pioneers. In the absence of social institutions and a unifying public opinion, a vigorous individualism branched into a great variety of character. Yankee independence has its roots in such a formative period, and it is incredible that a people, free for all the cranks and quirks of human nature, was ever chargeable with uniform goodness. Within a limited region—which has supplied the chief sources of historical tradition—a sifted population was molded by dominating men and effective institutions ; but beyond the pale of these ideal settlements there was a comfortable liberty, with only such sorting of men as results from the selection of the wilderness.

Our present theme forbids the attempt to trace the disintegration of character in the second and third generations in New England. This effect of the en-

vironing wilderness is unquestionable. It is but fair to
Dr. Bushnell to say that four years before he eulogized
the age of homespun, he described the descent towards
barbarism in these colonies in terms that were as accurate as they were graphic and startling.[1]   This
period, which he compared to that portrayed in the
Book of Judges, was succeeded by the Great Awakening, and later by the Revolution, so that before the
times over which he flung his enchantment were
reached, the people had passed through renewing fires.
We cannot fail to observe the fact—strengthening our
argument—that religion and war are alike in that they
exalt those who accept the call of duty, and are a savor
of death unto death to those who make a wrong response.   After times of regeneration the good are better and the bad are worse.   War, certainly, demoralizes
doubly, for beside the contagion of evil from massing
loose characters and the suspension of social restraints,
the bravest and best perish in disproportionate numbers
and the worthless save their lives.   There is little
reason to think that the inferior stratum of the population was either diminished or improved by the changes
of those critical times, and we are permitted to believe
that enough decadent folk passed into the age of homespun to preserve the stock to our own day.

The disparagement of the past implies a mean spirit.
We agree with Dr. Bushnell that " there is something
essentially bad in a people who despise or do not honor
their originals."   With him we exult in " that glorious
and auspicious distinction, that we have an ancestry

[1] Barbarism the First Danger, " Work and Play," pp. 240–245.

who after every possible deduction still overtop the originals of every nation of mankind—men fit to be honored and held in reverence while the continent endures." [1]   It is that possible—yea, necessary—deduction that is here pointed out.   There is no occasion to dim the lustre of the good; rather do we heighten it when it is represented as holding in check and vanquishing the bad.   The present suffers in comparison with the past because its evil is conspicuous and its good is a secret leaven, while in the past the bad are forgotten and the good are resplendent.   In the divine wisdom it is ordered that even the memory of the bad shall perish, and that as history lengthens there shall be an increasing galaxy of shining examples for the education of the race.   The charge that the country town is degenerate loses much of its force when a base line in the past is drawn with proper care. Much that seems degeneracy is the fruitage of earlier unfitness.   That it is low on the scale is not questioned; that it is a recent development in many cases is not denied.   The contention is that the truth of history is maintained and that the high interests of courage are served, if for the most part bad conditions in country towns are treated as an inheritance rather than a sudden acquisition.   The fate of such unfitness under natural selection has now to be considered.

[1] The True Wealth or Weal of Nations, "Work and Play," pp. 67, 69.

CHAPTER VIII

RURAL SELECTION

It is interesting to find in *The Spectator*, whose bi-centenary is but a few years in the future, a remark that might be an extract from the latest text-book of evolution: " A man, considered in his present state, seems only sent into the world to propagate his kind. He provides himself with a successor, and immediately quits his post to make room for him."[1] The most recent writers, it is true, do not insist upon immediate abdication, for it is now seen that the prolongation of life contributes an indispensable nurture to the rising generation, and that even the childless powerfully assist in the transfer of civilization by social heredity. Nevertheless evolution singles out for distinction the man who provides himself with a successor, and the number of successors which any class or society provides is deemed a critical test of social vitality.

The future of the rural community, as of every social group, depends upon the selection of persons who succeed in providing themselves with successors. We have seen what a heritage of the unfit lowers the present prosperity and vitality of the country town in all older sections of the land. If these unfit persons are to have successors, if they rather than fit persons are to be ancestors for later times, then degeneracy can be

[1] No. 111.

averted only by forces powerful enough to overcome
such base heredity. If, on the other hand, these unfit
persons are excluded from the genetic stream, there is
a fair prospect that the coming countryman will show
improvement. Natural selection has a fair field in the
rural population,—not indeed such a field as when
famine and plague and war thinned the race, but yet a
field that yields notable changes in the lines of human
development. More important than the selection by
death is the selection by emigration. They who go
out from a community leave no successors in it. This
is the chief factor in rural selection and merits attention beyond everything else. The questions to be an-
swered are sufficiently simple: Do the unfit die without children? Do they emigrate and leave no descendants in the country town?

In the broad view the unfit perish without contrib-
uting their equal share to after generations; they are
crushed out in the fierce struggle for existence. The
rural community in the hard conditions of the industrial revolution is an ideal field for this crowding to the
wall. The conspicuous fact is overpopulation. Where
there are too many people for the means of subsistence,
natural selection works automatically, as the weaker
elements of the population perish. Such is the general principle, and there is no doubt that under such
conditions, if men were animals, the unfit would perish
in such numbers as to restore equilibrium and definitely modify the species. Just how far this purging
takes place in human society, it is impossible to tell.
In two particulars man differs from animals, for he has

a higher intelligence and a superior morality. Were these distinguishing elements lacking, the result in the case of two thousand persons struggling for life in conditions adapted to the maintenance of fifteen hundred, would not be doubtful—some hundreds would come to a premature death, many of them before providing successors. It cannot be supposed that human intelligence and morality have been able to prevent a considerable destruction of unfit persons under this severe pressure of the environment. Distressing as is the death of the unfit, interpreted socially it promises the uplift of the race, gives assurance of a finer type of man, sets before the eager eye the earthly millennium. If natural selection could have unrestricted opportunity for its painful but fruitful work, the human species would be favorably modified even in a few generations, and the rural population would share richly in the costly improvement.

The unfit, however, are not killed off in this ruthless fashion anywhere within the bounds of Christian morality. The change from the merciless destruction to the compassionate preservation of the weak antedates Christianity. The most conspicuous charity in history is the feeding of the Roman populace from the public stores. Behind this mammoth mercy is an expulsion of the people from the land by the formation of great estates and the spread of Italian slavery. The horde of the disinherited was not suffered to starve. Something like this appears in English history. The early factory acts and the revised poor laws mark the same decade. By 1834 the burden of pauperism, which even two hundred years ago was as great relatively as at present,[1] had become so enormous that the method of dealing with it had to be changed. Here again behind the desperate treatment of appalling misery is a social tragedy. The new age of machinery dealt the rural population a heavy blow. Emigration could not afford relief at once, for only a part of the excess of labor could crowd into the cities, which were then in the experimental stage of their industrial development. Meanwhile the sentiments of mercy and the public conscience demanded the preservation of life. In a single day England and Wales have sometimes fed more than a million paupers.[2] A wiser administration has checked the growth of dependence; yet it is a fair question whether the vast increase of pauperism during the first half of the last century was not an inevitable consequence of the industrial revolution. The adjustment to the new environment could not be made at once, and human sympathy proved strong enough to preserve the inferior at a cost that threatened the very life of civilization. Relief finally came through the thinning out of the rural population and the concentration in cities, where new forms of labor gave support to the dislodged multitudes. Emigration to foreign countries cleared away other parts of a superfluous population, and after many decades of severe readjustment, that depleted condition, over which many have ignorantly lamented, was reached.

[1] The American Cyclopædia, " Pauperism."
[2] Johnson's Universal Cyclopædia, " Pauperism."

The experience of Great Britain makes plain the good fortune of the United States. Our people had the advantage of a high degree of mobility from the beginning,—being free to go where they pleased without hindrance from blundering laws. Vast unoccupied territories have invited settlement; a wise national administration has encouraged the formation of homesteads on new lands; the cities have offered countless opportunities for every grade of ability. The result is that a considerable part of the national domain has never had a larger population than it could support, and that the crowded districts have been able to find relief without a period of congestion issuing in huge burdens of pauperism. Four hundred thousand paupers, the number as estimated in 1890, is a slight load for the United States compared with twice as many for Great Britain with not half our population.[1] But let all croakers who cannot be reconciled to the depletion of the country town reflect upon the fact that our civilization had come to the parting of the ways, of which one was the reduction of vast numbers of the people to pauperism; the other the emigration of about one-fourth of the population wherever the homespun system had been fully established.

If the bars could have been put up,—the birth rate being maintained and private and public charity being excluded,—in the conditions that existed, there would have been such a destruction of the unfit as would have advanced the rural population many stages. If the bars had been put up,—with almshouses and

[1] Johnson's Universal Cyclopædia, "Pauperism."

charities in full operation and the birth rate maintained,—there would have been such an overloading of the strong with the care of the weak as would have made competition of the more densely populated states with the sparsely settled West impossible. The argument is not impaired by the seeming excess of the means of subsistence in the country town which out of its surplus contributes to the feeding of the city, for these supplies which are set apart for exchange for other commodities are as if they did not exist for the part of the community for which there is no employment. Fortunately the bars have been down, and those who were no longer useful in the new organization of industry have shifted for themselves; doubtless many have perished in the struggle before a foothold could be gained elsewhere. To-day public charity cares for comparatively few except the old, the infirm, the defective, and the children who are orphaned. Intemperance adds a few wrecks in middle life. Public charity now entails upon the future an unfit stock only to a very limited extent. To care for the aged is a harmless mercy; the almshouse in which births were frequent would not be tolerated; the care of the orphan is almost the only case in which charity influences the next generation. Under wise public care the orphan is by no means a hopeless ward, for often the stock is good, and even a base heredity yields to environment. The accepted policy is to place these children in good homes, and reared there they cease to be links in an evil chain.

The unfit are not crushed to death in great numbers;

they are not preserved alive by charity to any great extent: what then becomes of them? Upon the answer to that question depends the future of the rural population. If they emigrate, they are cleared away as effectually as by death. This would be a rural selection which would act far more rapidly and with a far higher potency for progress than natural selection working through death. It is interesting, at least, to ask what would be the improvement of the rural stock if year by year and decade by decade the unfit could be forced to emigrate. The pace of development would be quickened, and a superior type of humanity would appear in half a century. The limit would be fixed only by the rural environment. That, of course, could not be transcended; but of every environment men are a chief element, and these nobler men of higher intelligence would constitute an ideal society, quite capable of making the wilderness blossom as the rose. Paradise is always in the country, although the New Jerusalem is a city. The difficulty, of course, would be that cities of worthless refugees would loom ominously on the horizon; such a separation of classes would be the ruin of the world, in which even a rural paradise would share.

We claim no such purgation of the country at the expense of the city. On the contrary, we acknowledge that the reduction of the rural population takes place in a quite different way. We will let the pessimist state his interpretation. In his view the country town is a field for " Darwinism reversed," in which we have " natural selection the other end to—the survival of the unfittest."[1] The claim is that the best emigrate and leave the country to the unfit. In the absence of the most active and most competent, the inefficient are relieved from the pressure of competition and sink into an inert and dull existence, and these degenerates propagate an ever degenerating species. The country town is regarded as an isolated bit of quiescence where the unfit may live without disaster, though in consistency such an account must drop the term unfit, since these dull incompetents are perfectly adapted to the environment in which they stagnate.

Farther on there will be much to say of the rural environment and its influence; here we deal with the incidence of selection. Do the best or the worst emigrate? Or is such a mixture drained off as leaves the rural population vigorous and progressive? The gravity of the situation only a trained evolutionist can appreciate. President Jordan has pointed out the relation of war to national decadence with great vividness. Incidentally he remarks that the emigration of the best works in the same fatal way. Quoting Kipling's line,

"Send forth the best ye breed,"

he says : " This is Kipling's cynical advice to a nation which happily can never follow it. But could it be accepted literally and completely, the nation in time would breed only second-rate men. By the sacrifice of their best, or the emigration of the best, and by

[1] Rollin Lynde Hartt, " A New England Hill Town," *The Atlantic Monthly*, Vol. LXXXIII, p. 572.

such influences alone, have races fallen from first-rate to second-rate in the march of history."[1] In the crushed and spiritless "Man of the Hoe" he sees the type of that degenerate peasantry which is inevitable wherever the best are not retained.[2]

Relief from the dismal prospect portrayed by the despairing evolutionist cannot be found by denying the familiar fact that the most ambitious, the most energetic, the most intellectual, the most competent of the people leave the country to find a more congenial home in the city. Nor are restless energy and a dominating personality the chief forces to remove the best of the people from farm and hamlet. In the old times of isolation and independence one community was not much more important than another. In any thrifty town the three learned professions might be followed by their foremost representatives. We do, in fact, find famous preachers and theologians serving rural congregations; cultured and able physicians satisfied with a country practice; lawyers of high standing gracing the simple society of the village. And around such men gathered the courteous gentlemen of the old school.[3] Men of rare

[1] David Starr Jordan, "The Blood of the Nation," p. 11.

[2] *Ibid.*, p. 22.

[3] "He was a model of those formal but reverend manners which make what is called a gentleman of the old school, so called under an impression that the style is passing away, but which, I suppose, is an optical illusion, as there are always a few young men to whom these manners are native." Emerson of Samuel Hoar, Riverside Ed., Vol. X, p. 416. The suggestion of an optical illusion is more cheerful than convincing.

intelligence and virtue remained on the farms, for there was nothing else for them. Young men of promise and ambition were limited to a choice between the frontier and the sea. Almost any country town of the old time could furnish a judge for the county or a governor for the state. All this is changed. Men of superior ability are drawn to the cities by an irresistible attraction. Their removal is a necessity of the age, for the country town is impoverished that brain power may be centralized.

Decisive as are the evidences of this change in the distribution of superior persons, the extent of it may be exaggerated. One has only to recall the customary order of biographical sketches to realize that few of the leading men of the world have lived and died in the places of their birth. Country towns have seen the choicest of their sons and the fairest of their daughters forsaking their early homes ever since Abraham departed from Chaldea and Rebekah left her father's flocks in Mesopotamia. Aristotle remained in Stagira only long enough to immortalize his birthplace; Cicero found no field for his eloquence in his native Arpinum; Eislaben did not retain Luther beyond childhood; Corsica was quickly outgrown by Napoleon; Stratford, more fortunate, received her Shakespeare on his retirement from London. Genius gravitates to the university, the court, the metropolis. Other youths unknown to fame have taken the same road of ambition to Athens and Rome, to Paris and London and New York. History proves that there may be a considerable emigration of the choicest of

the people without injury to the community, so prolific of excellence is the human race. What is pointed
out in the depleted town is not so much the loss of
extraordinary persons as the removal little by little of
that highest stratum of the population from which
every kind of excellence is bred. It is not until
emigration goes beyond the universal drift to the
cities and the normal shiftings of residence that it
becomes significant. How far the industrial revolution
has broken down the higher circles of rural society, it
is impossible to say. Some observers tell of towns in
which " the fine old families " have quite disappeared.
In a multitude of cases farm and village houses have
fallen to occupants of a lower grade ; the foreigner, as
tenant or owner, cultivates lands that once paid the
parish tax and sent favored sons to college. So many
of these foreigners—to say nothing of inferior natives
—have pressed into the places of the homespun aristocracy that it is impossible to question that the ranks
of that old rural nobility are seriously thinned.

If this emigration of the best were the whole story,
it would be impossible to refute the charge of degeneracy. There is, however, another aspect of the
matter. The industrial revolution has put a pressure
upon rural life that is more important even than the
attraction of cities. That pressure has aggravated the
severity of the struggle for existence, and this grinding
of the mill of evolution has crushed the weaker strata
of the population. Among those who have gone are
laborers and their families, the owners and occupants
of the poorest lands—the famous abandoned farms,

and the weaklings and dependents. Many of these
have swollen the crowds of the factory towns ; others
have supplied unskilled labor to the cities; in not a
few cases they have gone to their destruction in the
slums, where residues of decadent folk finally disappear. Intemperance—to cite the most striking part
of the movement—has almost cured itself as a social
disease in the country. The drinkers first drank up
their farms ; then they and their families drifted. One
has only to ask an octogenarian concerning the families of his boyhood to learn what a sad number have
vanished through drink. Of these some were good
families, but more were of the inferior sort. The
human material that was most susceptible to alcohol
has gone into the mills of the gods. When all is
summed up, the clearance at the bottom is not less
significant than the loss at the top of the social scale.
Natural selection works as effectually in toning up the
species by weeding out the worst as " natural selection
reversed " works for degeneracy through the removal
of the best. This purgation has been overlooked ;
whether it offsets the injury in the highest stratum is a
fair question, but obviously no man is wise enough to
answer it. The opinion may be hazarded that when
the two influences are compounded, it will be found
that the average child has moved but a little way up or
down the scale. This is a local question to which
there are as many answers as communities.

The net result of these changes is a gain in homo-
geneousness ; in the country town the dream of equality
is nearer realization to-day than ever before. Once

each town had its Napoleonic financier for whose
shrewdness the neighbors were no match. These rural
accumulators of mortgages have gone to the city to
traffic with their peers. The country town is no
longer at their mercy. Such men were out of place
in the country,—it being better that neighbors who do
business with one another should meet on equal terms.
Something like this may be said of many kinds of
superiority. The most helpful citizen is one who is
not too far in advance of his fellows, and the most
wholesome society is that in which there is no select
circle to frown upon and dishearten all others. A half
dozen superior families give a town distinction, but
they may monopolize social opportunity. Their removal—though the loss is irreparable from other
points of view—gives an open field to those upon
whom new social responsibility falls. Those real
leaders,—superior to their fellows but not too far in
advance of them,—without whom a community fails
of its best life, are rightly mourned, if they depart; but
to a surprising degree their virtues and their abilities
are replaced by the rising up of other men and women
to fill the void. But what is here in mind is not wise
leadership but that aristocracy that blocks progress—
that unquestionable superiority which will neither enter nor suffer others to enter the kingdom. Often it is
a boon to a community to lose those whose commission
of social leadership served only to make it impossible
for others to accomplish anything for the public good.
The passing of the infidel squire may mean a new opportunity for religious faith; the vanishing of the fine

old gentlemen who went to the district school with complete content brings the educational reconstruction nearer ; radical reorganization of the rural churches waits for the departure of lingering saints. It is charteristic of every aristocracy that finally it can see nothing beyond its own tradition. Hence progress demands a rude shaking of quiescence and content, and paradoxical as it may seem, the departure of those known as the best people may be a social benefit. New England survived the loss of the Tories, and her interests were safe in the keeping of the less cultivated sons of liberty. That experience should teach all believers in democracy that it is never possible to tell in advance what high human qualities are forming where in the mediocrity of the time the mighty forces of equality and fraternity are at work. The like-mindedness essential to democracy may prove to be the unexpected but most welcome gift of depletion to country towns.

Be the balance of profit and loss what it may, nothing in history is plainer than the instability of a superior class. Mr. Pearson gives a vivid account of the rapid change in the English aristocracy, in which he finds only five families with no break in the male line to the fifteenth century. He cites the estimate that in 1825 only forty-eight of one hundred and fifty-five families went back to the First Parliament of James II. " The broad result," he says, " appears to be that left to itself from 1688 with new creations absolutely forbidden, the House of Lords would by this time have been practically extinguished." [1] It need excite no

[1] Charles H. Pearson, " National Life and Character," pp. 70–73.

alarm that the old aristocracy of our country towns succumbs to the fate that overwhelms all the aristocracies of the world. The more important question is whether other families are being bred to take their place,—whether it will be possible to name new peers of these noble men who will honor the rank to which they are elevated. It must be conceded that many country towns, for better or for worse, must get on without leaders descended from the foremost families of the old time. If a vigorous society remains, although under new leadership, it is possible that being set free from the weight of the weakest elements of the population, it may adjust itself to the conditions of the present age, and catching the movement of progress, advance with the swift development of modern civilization. In the worst possible outcome we may fall back upon Matthew Arnold's view that "a certain approach to equality, at any rate a certain reduction of signal inequalities, is a natural, instinctive demand of that impulse which drives society as a whole,—no longer individuals and limited classes only but the mass of a community,—to develop itself with the utmost possible fullness and freedom." [1] And when selection has sifted the rural community most severely, there remains, if we have observed its incidence correctly, a population that answers to Aristotle's ideal: "But a city ought to be composed, as far as possible, of equals and similars ; and these are generally the middle classes." [2]

[1] " Mixed Essays," p. 10.   (Democracy.)
[2] " The Politics of Aristotle," Jowett, Vol. II, p. 127.

CHAPTER IX

THE PRESSURE OF THE IMMIGRANT

At this point it becomes necessary to take note of a grand disturbance in the course of rural development which we are considering. History is never simple, and we no sooner think we have mastered the secret of its movement than new facts throw our premature explanations into confusion. Depletion of the country population and its causes are sufficiently plain; thus far all seems consistent, but unfortunately for our peace of mind, portentous facts hitherto overlooked force themselves upon attention. We have endeavored to account for the rural exodus; meanwhile there is discovered a rural immigration that seems to contradict our interpretation. Why should an alien people in threatening numbers invade overcrowded country towns? And if they persist in forcing an entrance, what will be the result? The pressure of the immigrant calls for careful consideration.

The paradox confronts us that over population gives the foreigner his opportunity in country towns. In the competition whose issue is the exodus of the superfluous, the foreigner takes a hand; the severe conditions of the industrial revolution, to which native families cannot adjust themselves, offer the invader precisely the opportunity that suits those whose

standard of living is low.   In certain kinds of competition cheapness has the advantage.   Poor lands call
for cheap men ; in hard times the better farms demand
cheap families ; and when it seems impossible to make
the ends meet, a cheap laborer is welcomed.   Ultimately a difficult environment requires and develops
better men ; the immediate advantage passes to
cheaper men.   The foreigner, therefore, finds his
opportunity where others fail, and this displacement
of the native stock by the immigrant is a most serious
element in the rural situation.

The problem of population is far too complex for
solution by this simple economic principle.   More
important than the crowding out of the adult native
is the influence upon the birth rate in the native
stock.   There is here that typical competition in
which the unborn contend for the privilege to live
which marks the evolutionary process under natural
selection.   President Francis A. Walker has expressed
the belief that additions to the population by immigration have prevented the natural increase in native
families, so that instead of a reenforcement of our
population there has been merely a substitution of
foreign for native stock.[1]   In his opinion the shock to
the birth rate is moral rather than physical,—those
accustomed to a high standard of living being un-
willing to bring sons and daughters into the world to
suffer the degradation of competition under these
hopeless conditions.   He supports his view by a care-

[1] " Discussions in Economics and Statistics," Vol. II, pp. 420–426.
Cf. pp. 120–124.

ful analysis of the statistics of population. From 1790 to 1830—when immigration was so slight as to be disregarded—the population increased at the unprecedented rate of 227 per cent. in four decades. Between 1830 and 1850, immigrants to the number of 2,312,000 were added to the population, and the births from the native stock fell off to an equal extent from the famous estimate of Elkanah Watson, which was based on the rate of increase from 1790 to 1810. By 1890, 12,-971,842 additional immigrants had come,[1] with the result that the total population was 14,644,739 less than Watson's prediction. It is evident, therefore, that the birth rate received a severe shock at the time of the foreign invasion, and it is a striking coincidence, at least, that the failure of the native stock to make good its early promise corresponds so closely to the pressure of the immigrant.

Alluring as is potential history, it is never quite safe to say what would have been if things had been different. It is not easy to be reconciled to the substitution of a motley and mongrel population for that homogeneous people of one blood that might have filled the land, if this reasoning were well founded. It is not certain that the loss is as great as this speculation represents, for the birth rate was certain to be checked as the country filled up. The conditions that gave free expansion to population in the early period had changed radically by 1850. That date brings to mind the industrial revolution, the excess of the rural population, and the increasing stress of competition.

[1] Supplied from Twelfth Census, U. S., Vol. I, p. cii.

The crowding of native upon native would have altered the birth rate, so that expectations based upon the early rate of natural increase could not have been realized under any circumstances. On the one hand the shock to the birth rate from the competition of native with native would have been less severe, but on the other hand native parents would have shrunk from rearing large families for the rougher kinds of work. It is probable that without immigration the population of the country would have been some millions less than it now is, although it would have been many millions more than the present native stock numbers. Certainly the common assertion that without the foreigner the development of the country would have halted disastrously is fallacious.

The decline in the birth rate during the nineteenth century has such adequate explanation in the prudential and moral adjustment to changed economic conditions that it is unnecessary to search for more obscure causes. As much confusion, however, results from the riot of exaggeration, as from false interpretations, in current views of the decadence of the native stock. Prior to 1830 the rate of natural increase was phenomenal—" never known before or since among any considerable population, over any extensive region," as President Walker says. The falling off from that extraordinary rate is not greater than can be accounted for without resort to the hypothesis of physical infertility. It is worth while at some cost of patience to gain a correct view of the stability of the native stock.

Dr. Edward Jarvis, the first president of the American Statistical Association, rendered an important service in pointing out the fallacies of earlier writers.[1] Mr. Louis Schade seems to have been the decoy of the statisticians. He computed the increase of the population of 1790 on the assumption of a uniform rate of 1.38 per cent. annually,—the rate that he thought he ascertained for the natural increase of population from 1850 to 1851.[2] Mr. Friedrich Kapp, adopting this method, found that in 1865 there were 9,034,245 descendants of the people enumerated in the first census. This number subtracted from the total population gave 20,965,755 persons of foreign extraction. The paper containing this colossal blunder, which had already had a career of thirteen years, was read before the American Social Science Association as late as 1869.[3] If it is true, as has been suggested, that the function of statistics is the refutation of other statistics, there could be no better example of their necessity. In this case the error was not confined to learned societies, but it became current as a popular misapprehension. To this day it survives in the common impression that the descendants of those persons who were in the United States in 1790 —the natives and the native stock as the terms are used throughout this discussion—are comparatively few, and that the immigrants since 1790 and their descendants—the foreigners and the foreign stock as

---

[1] *Atlantic Monthly*, Vol. XXIX, pp. 454–468. (April, 1872.)
[2] " The Immigration into the United States of America."
[3] " European Emigration to the United States."

the terms are here applied—constitute the mass of the population. At the risk of provoking incredulity, the immense fruitfulness of the native stock must be made apparent,—a fruitfulness so great as to make President Walker's contention that the land could have been peopled without the foreigner entirely sane.

If the native and foreign stocks were marked like the whites and the blacks, there would be no difficulty in determining their relative number. They are, of course, inextricably crossed and confounded, so that they cannot be separated nor enumerated. The census proceeds upon the patriotic assumption that all whose grandparents were born in this country are of one sort,—separately enumerating only the foreign-born and the children of the foreign-born. The data for our problem are the number of immigrants in each decade and the gain of the white population, from which the per cent. of increase of the white population in each decade can be computed. It is then possible on the basis of the known population in 1790 to calculate the number of persons of this native stock at each census year. By this method Dr. Jarvis concluded that in 1870 the number of whites of foreign descent was 11,607,394, and that the number of native descent was 21,479,595. Professor Richmond Mayo-Smith brought the computation down to the time of writing his book "Emigration and Immigration," though with less exact determination of some details. He reached the result that in 1880 the whites of foreign descent numbered eighteen millions, and the whites of native descent about twenty-five and one-half millions. He estimated that in 1888 the two elements of the population were respectively twenty-five and twenty-nine millions.[1] The immigration from 1880 to 1890 proved to be unprecedented, and the result of the computation from the statistics is twenty-six millions of foreign and twenty-nine millions of native descent in 1890.[2] Ten years later the two elements of the white population had become substantially equal,—each numbering thirty-three and one-half millions, if this mode of calculation is followed. This, however, is only an approximate computation, for the painstaking of Dr. Jarvis is scarcely worth while on account of a source of error which must now be pointed out.

It is assumed by Dr. Jarvis that the rate of increase, computed for the whole white population, applies with equal accuracy to the native and foreign stocks. It is the common belief that the population of foreign descent has increased much more rapidly than the native stock. It is wholly impossible to verify this conjecture. All that is known from the census is that a little less than twenty-six millions of the white population are certainly of foreign descent,—being foreign born or children of the foreign-born,—and that a little more than forty-one millions have parents who were born in this country. According to the mode of computation adopted by Dr. Jarvis, of the last, seven and

<hr>

[1] "Emigration and Immigration," pp. 59, 60.

[2] In a later work, by the same author, "Statistics and Sociology," p. 328, the correction here suggested is made.

one-half millions are of foreign descent,—their grandparents or remoter ancestors being immigrants since
1790. Undoubtedly this number is too small, but if it
is increased to any probable extent,-it will be so small
a part of forty-one millions that the population of native descent is demonstrably increasing. In 1870 there
could have been no considerable error in Dr. Jarvis's
estimate, since at that time the third and fourth generations were not largely represented in the immigrant
families, and the native birth rate had been well maintained during several of the decades in question. Assuming the approximate accuracy of the computation
of the natives as numbering 21,479,595 in 1870, no possible falling off from thirty-three and one-half millions
—the estimate for 1900—could make the gain of the native stock anything less than substantial, if not imposing.

The stability of the native stock will appear, if we
apply an extreme supposition. The limit of possibility
in the natural increase of the foreign stock is far
below the rate of thirty-three and one-third per cent.
for each of the last three decades. This is approximately the rate for the increase of the native stock
during the phenomenal period from 1790 to 1820,
when the per cent. was 35.1, 36.4, and 33.1 for the
several decades.[1] Starting with 11,607,394 persons of
foreign descent in 1870—the estimate of Dr. Jarvis—
the foreign stock increasing naturally one-third each
decade and augmented by the actual inflow from
abroad would have numbered approximately forty-six
millions in 1900. This deducted from the total white

[1] Twelfth Census, U. S., Vol. I, p. xxv.

population leaves twenty-one millions for the native
stock. Under this extreme and altogether improbable
supposition the result is reached that the native stock
failed to keep its twenty-one and one-half millions intact by only an insignificant fraction. The truth probably lies somewhere between Dr. Jarvis's assumption
of an equal rate of increase for the foreign and native
stocks, and this extreme proposition that the native
stock is stationary while the foreign stock repeats the
marvel of native fecundity in the early period from
1790 to 1820. There is no possible way of determining
the facts until the census enumerates all persons in
whose blood is a strain of the immigrant. One man's
guess is as good as another's, and, perhaps, the chief
value of this discussion is in bringing to light the impossibility of finding statistical support for the persist-
ent assertion that the native stock is decadent. If we
cannot prove positively that it increases, we can be absolutely sure that no man can demonstrate that it de-
creases. The stability of the native stock is overwhelmingly probable.

Even in New England the case is by no means desperate. Rev. Calvin E. Amaron, formerly president
of the French American College in Springfield, Mass.,
has set in impressive and startling array some of the
facts in the rapid transformation of the New England
population. He has compiled, also, from the newspapers of this section expressions of alarm at the situation.[1] The point of interest and anxiety is the coming

[1] "Your Heritage in New England Threatened." See especially
pp. 28-48.

predominance of the foreigner. We are compelled to concede that the native stock is already outnumbered. In 1900 the foreign population of the first and second generations alone was fifty-four per cent. of the whole;[1] if we add the unknown numbers descended from earlier immigrants, it is apparent that the old stock is but a fraction of the people in the section where its history is long and honorable. There is no question that the immigration into New England is phenomenal and threatening, and that prolific invaders strike at the stability of the older population with unprecedented vigor. President Amaron cites an example of a French Canadian who lived until his descendants numbered seven hundred. With no small trepidation we inquire how the native stock stands the pressure.

Unfortunately the data for a demonstration that the native stock of New England continues to reproduce itself are not available, for the statistics that might be helpful are merged in those of the nation. It is possible, however, by special computations to discover what is known and where uncertainty begins. In the census tables the last decade shows a gain in the six New England states of 75,318 in the native whites of native parentage.[2] It would seem, therefore, that the native stock and the foreign stock of native parentage together maintain their numbers with a good margin, and that we have only to estimate the relative productivity of the two strains in the population to reach the facts concerning the fertility of the native stock.

[1] Computed from Twelfth Census, U. S., Vol. I, p. clxxxii.

[2] *Ibid.*, p. 489.

This promise of an easy solution melts into uncertainty as we reflect upon the extent of the migration of all classes of the people across the border of New England in either direction. The increase of the native whites of native parentage is not a secure starting point until corrected for this movement. Incidentally it appears from the investigation of this matter that the tide has turned so that New England is now receiving more people than she sends out, exclusive of the foreign-born. As this fact is contrary to the common impression, there is an aditional reason for presenting the result of a very laborious and perplexing computation.

Residents of New England born in states outside of New England :—

[1]Enumerated in 1890 - - 207,496
[2]Of these there were living in 1900 170,416
[3]Enumerated in 1900 - - - 308,301
Newly enumerated in 1900 - 137,885

Residents of states outside of New England born in New England :—

[4]Enumerated in 1890 - - - 551,460
Of these there were living in 1900 452,915
Enumerated in 1900 - - 524,979

[1] Computed from Eleventh Census, Vol. I, p. cxii.
[2] Average annual death rate 18.7, Twelfth Census, Vol. III, p. lvi.
[3] Computed from Twelfth Census, Vol. I, p. cxxxvi.
[4] Computed from Eleventh Census, Vol. I, p. cxxii.

Newly enumerated in 1900 - -	72,064
Added to New England from interstate migration during last decade - - - - -	65,821
[1] Children born after arrival of parents - - - - -	13,528
Total increase from these two sources - - - -	79,349
[2] Deduct 7,000 colored - - -	72,349
[3] Those of native parentage approximate sixty per cent. of native whites, equal - - -	43,309

One correction should be made in the foregoing estimate. Some 7,000 persons went out of New England to meet death before 1900, if we suppose that those going during the decade were evenly distributed through the ten years; of these 4,000 may have been whites of native parentage. The gain to New England from 1890 to 1900 through interstate migration, therefore, reduces to approximately 40,000 whites of native parentage, and there remain 35,000 native whites of native parentage to be accounted for by natural increase. The most that can be claimed for this estimate is that error arising from its assumptions where data are lacking and from the failure to trace the incidence of births and

[1] Supposed to equal the death losses of a population yielding 137,885 survivors in 1900, averaging a residence of five years.

[2] Excess above average rate of increase for the United States, Twelfth Census, Vol. I, pp. cxii, cxiii.

[3] Exactly 61.4 per cent. in New England. *Ibid.*, pp. clxxxvi and 489.

deaths in the migrating hosts—a matter of bottomless perplexity—cannot blot out the margin of 35,000 on the side of the stability of the two strains of the New England stock of native parentage when taken together.

Recurring now to the question of the vitality of the old stock dating from 1790, it is clear that on the assumption of equal birth and death rates in the native and foreign strains, each approximately reproduced itself during the last decade. The probability is that the foreign stock had a slightly higher rate in deaths and in births, which would allow the native stock to keep its numbers intact with the lower birth rate. Inasmuch as the belief in the superior fertility of the foreign stock undoubtedly exceeds the facts, it may be worth while to say that if the rate of natural increase exhibited by the native stock from 1790 to 1810 had been duplicated in every decade by the foreign stock of New England, the foreign stock of native parentage would have been numerous enough to have provided for the replacement of its own death losses and the death losses of more than a million and a half of the native stock, that would have been in existence even on this assumption. Were this assumption true, not a child could have been born of the native stock for a decade without being smuggled in through the indefinite margins of a statistical approximation. When the actual number of children born of the native stock is considered, it becomes clear that one cannot go very far in affirming a superior birth rate in the foreign stock of the third and fourth generations without pillorizing himself on a reductio ad absurdum. The probability is that when immigrants have lived with us so long that their grandparents were born in the land, there is little more difference between the two stocks in reproductivity than between any other equally extensive groups taken at random. If one chooses to be a little reckless—and undoubtedly the assertion is not quite safe—he may boldly declare that the native New England stock is now reproducing itself; and he may do this in absolute confidence that the data do not exist that will enable any one to refute the claim. But not to throw down the gauntlet rashly, it may be said that at the utmost the New England stock falls but a little below the number of births required to make good the losses by death.

It is difficult to avoid the pitfalls of this subject. The vital statistics, especially, deceive the unwary. The large number of deaths of natives is often construed as indicating the decadence of the old families. Thus under the title, " The Decline of Yankees in New England," [1] such facts are culled from the vital statistics of Connecticut for 1899 as that " the registered mortality was 14,381, of whom more than 10,000 were natives." Before drawing the inference that " these figures show that the young people have struck out into, new regions, leaving the old folks behind them," who are presumed to furnish the victims of mortality, allowance should be made for the high death rate among children of the foreign stock. In

[1] *World's Work*, June, 1901.

the usage of the vital statistics every child born in this country is a native,[1] and it is notorious that infant mortality is exceptionally great in immigrant families in consequence of parental incompetence and the change of environment. The excess of deaths of natives over the births from native parents, as shown in the vital statistics, is absolutely worthless as evidence of racial decadence.

In view of all these considerations,—adduced to show what the problem is and serving to reveal the futility of current arguments rather than as demonstrations where proof is impossible because of the lack of data,—it seems justifiable to proceed in the general discussion on the basis that the native stock is stable, though no longer yielding a natural increase, in New England, and that it is growing slowly in the country as a whole. The native stock is destined to be a minority wherever immigration pours its hordes into the land, but that minority will not waste nor diminish; it is a leaven, pervasive, vital, lasting. The invasion of the foreigner is by no means as ominous as it would be if he pressed into a vacuum created by the decay of a wasting race. The ground is yielded voluntarily by a virile people seeking more favorable conditions. If the native stock does not remain in the country towns, it must still be reckoned with in the nation as a whole, and it may be trusted to dominate the

---

[1] The reader is advised again that throughout this discussion the native stock is the descendants of the persons enumerated in the census of 1790, and that the foreign stock includes all others,—an arbitrary and awkward, but, it is hoped, intelligible use of terms.

entire population and permeate it ultimately with its own ideals. Taking the East and the West together, it is not at all improbable that the native stock in country towns will never be less than it is to-day; in New England and the older sections the indications are that the foreign stock will make slow gains at the expense of the old rural families.

The substitution of the foreigner for the native in the rural towns need not, as yet, occasion serious concern. In New Hampshire, whose percentage of foreign population is not quite nine-tenths that of all New England,—being two per cent. higher than that for the United States, without the colored population,—the composition of the population may be regarded as typical of the older section of the North. In the towns of this state which have less than 2,500 inhabitants, the foreign-born and those of foreign parentage are 24.5 per cent. of all the people; in the fifteen larger towns they are 40.1 per cent.; in the ten cities other than Manchester they are 46.9 per cent.; and in Manchester they are 71.3 per cent. of the whole population.[1] It may be conjectured that the foreign born and those of foreign parentage are four-fifths of all who are of foreign descent, as the term is used in this discussion, for in the computation of Dr. Jarvis they were thirty-nine fiftieths of all. The persons of foreign descent, then, would be 30.6 per cent. in the rural towns; 50.1 per cent. in the larger towns; 58.6 per cent. in the ten

[1] Computed from Twelfth Census, Vol. I, p. 665. The colored population is counted on the foreign side, numbering only 897 for the whole state.

cities; and 89.1 per cent. in Manchester. We have then the remarkable conclusion that in the rural towns two persons in three are more likely to be of the native stock than one person in ten in Manchester or two persons in five in the other cities. Plainly the foreign invasion, however important it may be in the country towns, primarily concerns the cities.

The assimilation of the foreigner is far more rapid in the rural communities, where he is outnumbered two to one; where he cannot provide himself with separate churches and schools; where every man knows his neighbor; where laborer and employer associate in the comradeship of the farm. The country town is fitted providentially for unique service in making a nation out of a vast conglomerate of peoples. In the process of assimilation the descendants of the early immigrants are a critical factor; upon the thoroughness of their transformation in a new environment depends the issue for the whole invasion. They came at a time when the full influence of our customs and institutions fell upon their isolated households, and their children, often indistinguishable from the native stock, are a solvent of incalculable efficiency in the digestion of what otherwise would be an overwhelming immigration.

Our conclusion differs from current, pessimistic views not in ignoring the extent of the foreign invasion nor in minimizing the shock experienced by the old rural population, but in seizing upon the two critical elements in the situation—the vitality of the native stock and the vast preparation for assimilating the immigrant host. Here and there the old families will disappear, —the old aristocracy we cannot hope to preserve; but in general enough of the original population will remain in the country towns to set a wholesome standard of life, to perpetuate the ancient ideals, and to dominate the incoming races.

This chapter treats the immigrant quantitatively only. After what has been said in an earlier chapter of the inheritance of unfitness, it should be unnecessary to say that an exchange of much native stock for immigrants would be a good bargain. The decade in which one crosses the Atlantic signifies as little as the stars under which he is born.

BOOK IV

THE DIRECT ACTION OF
ENVIRONMENT

" The environment of a community comprises all the circumstances, adjacent or remote, to which the community may be in any way obliged to conform its actions. It comprises not only the climate of a community, its soil, its flora and fauna, its perpendicular elevation, its relation to mountain-chains, the length of its coast-line, the character of its scenery, and its geographical position with reference to other countries; but it includes also the ideas, feelings, customs, and observances of past times, so far as they are preserved by literature, traditions, or monuments; as well as foreign contemporary manners and opinions, so far as they are known and regarded by the community in question."

—*John Fiske*, " *Cosmic Philosophy*," *Vol. II, p. 197.*

CHAPTER X

RECENT INTERPRETATIONS OF EVOLUTION

It is no part of the purpose of this book to discuss the laws of evolution, yet it seems necessary to pause here for a brief consideration of new points of view that promise great fruitfulness in the treatment of rural problems. Thus far we have regarded evolution as a process in which natural selection has a chief part, and we have endeavored to trace the incidence of selection as it affects the rural population. No adequate theory of evolution can ever dispense with natural selection, whatever other agencies are recognized; and certainly what we have termed rural selection has unmistakable influence in transforming the country people. Indeed the rapid change in the composition of the rural population by depletion and by the substitution of the immigrant for the native, forced the inquiry concerning this human sorting and suggested the submission of these local questions to the higher court of scientific evolution. Having appealed to this court, we are required to conduct the case in the light of all principles that it recognizes.

All evolutionists agree concerning the effect of eliminating those individuals of a species that fail of adjustment to their environment—that the survivors perpetuate their own stock and so far change the character

of the species.   It was Darwin's great merit to discern
the immediate and the remoter consequences of this
perfectly simple and unquestionable principle, and no
scientific evolutionist to-day thinks of constructing a
theory of development without large use of it.   To say
that adapted individuals survive in the struggle for existence slips easily over the greatest of difficulties, for the
problem is to account for the adapted individual.
Darwin supposed that slight differences—such as are
observable everywhere—were sufficient to give the in-
itial advantage and that selection accumulated them
into specific distinctions.   The weak link in the reasoning is that these petty variations would not be of use,
and evolutionists have sought in every conceivable way
to discover and account for variations great enough for
their purpose.

Present interest centres in the mutation theory of
De Vries, which has an able expositor in Professor
Thomas Hunt Morgan.[1]   This theory provides ample
variations at a stroke, for it teaches that besides
the fluctuations that distinguish the individuals of a
species from one another there are more radical
changes that set off certain individuals once for all to
become the progenitors of a new kind.   These kinds
appearing suddenly may be real species, or they may
be elementary species of which a few will be rated
species when the intermediate varieties have disappeared.   The mutation theory is advocated with such
use of technical details as forbids its explanation here
—much more its criticism.   In the chapter dealing

[1] "Evolution and Adaptation."

with personal forces facts will come into view upon which it seems to shed some light.

From the beginning there has been an undefined assumption that in some way the environment modifies individuals and thus gives rise to the variations that the theory of natural selection demands. This has been the popular belief. There came over into Darwinism a large inheritance from Lamarck, who clearly perceived the influence of environment upon the individual and the effects of the use and disuse of organs. Lamarck believed that these modifications could be transmitted to offspring; were this true, the accumulating modification through successive generations would provide the variation required for the working of the theory of evolution. More exact investigation has made it impossible to be confident that acquired qualities are inherited. Weismann has pronounced definitely against the inheritance of acquired qualities, but he has accounted for the likeness of child and parent in a way that leaves the matter practically much as it was believed to be before it was mystified by technical detail. The acquired quality gives the individual possessing it an advantage in the struggle for existence; the result is the preservation of this modified individual until offspring are produced which evince a predisposition towards the character first acquired by the parent. "Although natural selection appears to operate upon qualities of the developed organism alone, it in truth works upon peculiarities hidden in the germ-cells." [1]

[1] August Weismann, "Essays Upon Heredity," Vol. I, p. 104. For

The suggestion that the sifting of individuals also selects germinal peculiarities has pointed out a new path for evolutionary theories. It has only to be combined with the fundamental conception of Lamarckism, that the environment powerfully influences the individual, to be immensely fruitful for evolutionary speculation. If the environment has an influence under which living things are plastic to a considerable degree, then they may be so modified that they will gain the advantage that selects them for life; but in their selection their germinal elements live on also, and though the germ-plasm can never keep pace with the changes wrought by the environment, it will maintain its distance in the rear. The ultimate result is that characters acquired under the stimulus of environment appear in the genetic stream. They are never inherited, but finally they run in the blood of the generations. The modifications wrought by the direct action of the environment blaze the way, and the species follows on. This is the theory, known as "organic selection," advocated by many recent evolutionists and expounded definitely and authoritatively by Prof. J. Mark Baldwin in his book, " Development and Evolution."

As long as it was supposed that acquired qualities are inherited, it was necessary to reduce the volume of acquisition to some fair proportion to what seemed to be the actual inheritance of the offspring. The tendency, therefore, was to minimize the influence of

a summary of the theory of germinal selection, see Weismann's " The Germ Plasm," pp. 410–435.

environment. With a theory that demands a vastly greater influence of the environment than ever is manifest in the actual transformation of the species— individuals changing many degrees while the species changes a single degree—there is every incentive to study the direct action of the environment, and nothing stands in the way of its full potency. It is not true that species are plastic beyond what has always been discerned, but individuals are seen to be plastic beyond what has been believed. In the case of man, above all, the individual is molded by his environment,—a multitude of men anticipating the type ultimately developed by natural selection. In fact Professor Baldwin, approaching these problems of human evolution with a training in psychology rather than in biology, relies upon what he terms social heredity rather than upon physical inheritance. By social heredity he means the transformation of a succeeding generation into the likeness of its predecessors in consequence of the subjection of both generations to a similar environment, or by reason of the influence of the earlier upon the later generation. This, of course, is a direct action of environment, for by far the most important part of the environment of man is just this encompassing mass of men—their personalities, their institutions, their traditions, their educational systems, their literatures. Civilization passes from generation to generation by this social heredity, although it is favored by natural selection, which in the end will fill the earth with a race formed for civilization and living the civilized life as by instinct.

In sociology the plasticity of the individual is known as imitation; the influence of the environment as suggestion.

Even animals imitate to a surprising extent, and there is an education going forward in fields and woods and waters that deserves, in poetic license at least, the name of school. A naturalist, who has not escaped criticism for his remarkable observations, among many such fascinating tales gives a description of a caribou school.[1] In late summer five or six mothers were observed in the process of introducing their little ones to the society of their fellows. One may dismiss this instruction in social usages as a delightful fancy, but it is not so easy to dispose of the jumping lesson, which holds the chief place in the caribou curriculum. It is easy to read human meanings into animal performances, but in advance of observation it is perilous to set limits to learning by imitation. The roots of this controversy are in unlike estimates of a plastic and teachable individuality on the one hand and of the perfected instinct of the species on the other. Organic selection has more room for a " school of the woods " in its theory than Darwinism.

On the human level there can be no question concerning the part played by social heredity. Education is the definite use of this method, providing teachers, organizing opportunities, and utilizing to the utmost the plasticity of youth. All propagation of ideas, every kind of agitation with a view to the change of public opinion, the work of press, platform, and pul-

[1] William J. Long, " Wilderness Ways," pp. 16–21.

pit, have place in this system in which an environment of great power acts upon the plastic individual. The unconscious and unpremeditated transmission of these social influences is even more effective than intentional and organized efforts. The descent of most national traits from generation to generation could be accounted for in this way, although ultimately many of these characteristics are carried in the genetic stream, passing from parent to child by physical heredity.

The time must soon come, if it has not already arrived, when a really illuminating account of social development must be stated in the terms of evolution, as science traces it throughout the fields of life. In former chapters the argument rests upon the clear fact that evolution gains its most ample field among the varying multitudes of men, whose vast range in intellectual and social and moral and religious attainment presents to natural selection a unique diversity. And here it is not less evident that the interpretation of evolution that makes full use of the direct action of the environment upon the individual has peculiar interest in its application to man, for he is responsive to a far richer environment than other creatures, and with his boundless capacities is immeasurably more plastic than his associates in the common scheme of development. There is no occasion to disparage natural selection as the new principle comes into clearer light, yet if one must rank the agents in accordance with their actual service in the human field, the direct action of the environment upon the individual—made effective in the transformation of the species by organic selection

—may be set above Darwinian natural selection without injustice.

This conclusion yields a most valuable contribution to rural problems. The prospect for the rural population is far brighter than the observed working of selection suggests. Assuming, for the moment, that the best emigrate from the country town, it seems inevitable that the people should degenerate as new generations are bred from the inferior stock left behind. This need not be the case at all, if we have reached a true view of the method of evolution. A blighting but needless discouragement broods over the modern mind because the worse families have many, and the better families have few children. So great is the penalty of scientific misconception when the guarded opinions of scholars enter the popular mind through treacherous catch-words. The crucial fact is the power of environment,—which includes social heredity and education and every philanthropic force and all uplifts of democracy. More significant by far than the purging of natural selection, is the transformation of peoples by which worthless human stock is improved after it is born. The laws of evolution are such that ultimately improvements flow in the blood, and well-born children appear in lines springing from ignoble ancestors. This power of children to be better than the fathers is the key to history and the hope of sociology. There is no scientific reason for the popular notion that the depleted rural population is under a fatality of evil. Its future depends almost wholly upon the power of environment,—upon education, upon commerce, upon evangelization, upon participation in the great movements of the age. The best may go forth year by year, but if the forces that make men after they are born are in full vigor, the rural population will keep its place in the general progress of mankind.

Warning is not less mandatory than the summons to courage, for bad environments are prolific of evil. In his famous address, " Barbarism the First Danger," [1] Dr. Bushnell made a profound study of environments before the evolutionist had confused a simple matter. It was his view that migration detached a people from its old social environment with ominous consequences. The institutions, the customs, the refining influences of the old home cannot be immediately replaced. Hence in new lands degeneracy is inevitable in the first generations. Thus he saw it in his own day on the frontier; thus he read the early history of New England, whose second and third generations " were as if a nest of eagles had been filled with a brood of owls." Those born to be eagles became owls in the wilderness; and there is no doubt that an owl species would have succeeded in time, of which owls and owls only would have been born, if the environment had not been enriched as a new civilization grew into vigor; if the schools, the churches, the democratic institutions, the solemn and uplifting ideals of a high movement of humanity had not gained ascendancy over the debasing wilderness. The rural population is threatened with an impoverished environment in the changes

[1] " Work and Play," pp. 227–267.

of the times, but the danger should arouse all lovers and helpers of men as well as those in immediate peril to labor for that better environment of commerce and education and religion—that ceaseless influence of ideals and institutions—which is competent to develop eagles even from owls. Our investigation must now seek to ascertain the actual character of the rural environment.

CHAPTER XI

THE INFLUENCE OF NATURE

IT must be conceded that the incidence of selection is such that if nothing else acts upon the people who remain after the sifting of the rural population, degeneracy must ensue. At the best, humanity has a great root and a huge bulk of stalk and leaf for the few blossoms into which it flowers. If all the bloom is plucked repeatedly, how differs the choicest garden bed from the weeds of the roadside that fling no colors to the breeze? For the moment after the cutting it may seem that there is no difference, but next morning's sun will find the dewy garden ablaze again. There are secret forces at work that make the country competent year after year to send forth men and women who have the fine qualities of their predecessors. Among these helpful forces the influence of nature merits special attention.

We may borrow from Washington Irving a thesis for this chapter: " In rural occupation there is nothing mean and debasing. It leads a man forth among scenes of natural grandeur and beauty ; it leaves him to the working of his own mind, operated upon by the purest and most elevating of external influences. Such a man may be simple and rough, but he cannot be vulgar. The man of refinement, therefore, finds nothing revolting in an intercourse with the lower orders in rural life, as he does when he casually mingles with the lower orders of cities."[1]

It is common to speak of the love of nature as a very recent acquisition. It may recall us to a more seemly modesty if we read once more in *The Spectator* how the wise and good Aurelia and the husband, " who has been in love with her ever since he knew her, wresting themselves away from their walks and gardens, sometimes live in town, not to enjoy it so properly, as to grow weary of it, that they may renew in themselves the relish of a country life."[2] This was two generations before Cowper wrote more than a century ago :

> " The country wins me still;
> I never framed a wish, or formed a plan
> That flattered me with hope of earthly bliss,
> But there I laid the scene."[3]

The appreciation of nature is not a raw product of the latest enthusiasm ; it is a vintage of many seasons, and although the store is greater in recent years, mellow remainders still tell of the abundant flow of old-time presses. Where is there a finer expression of feeling for landscape than in Petrarch's lines ?

> " Once more, ye balmy gales, I feel you blow;
> Again, sweet hills, I mark the morning beams
> Gild your green summits; while your silver streams
> Through vales of fragrance undulating flow."[4]

[1] " The Sketch Book," Rural life in England.
[2] No. 15.
[3] " The Task," Book IV.
[4] Oscar Kuhns, " The Great Poets of Italy," p. 141.

Dante was a close observer of nature, particularly of the effects of light. With the glorious outburst of Italian song in the thirteenth and fourteenth centuries, the silence of voiceless times should not be cited as proof of the late development of the love of nature.

If the love of nature were of yesterday only, it would be too soon to look for effects in the character of the country people. The true account is that these refining forces act in all ages with impartial vigor, although their effect depends upon the feeling of the time and the sensitiveness of those upon whom they play. What we see in our day is the culmination in self-consciousness of this pressure of natural beauty upon men as they finally apprehend what has always haunted the recesses of feeling. None escape altogether the uplift of soul and the quieting of passion and the awakening of the friendly spirit and the discipline of patience, as day after day they live in the presence of the mighty hills or within the vast rim of the prairie, and night by night witness the solemn march of the stars, and year in and year out pay the unchanging price of labor for the bounty of the fields. Knowing how these influences of nature penetrate the heart and mold the character, we share the feeling which Webster expressed before the rise of cities: " I am not anxious to accelerate the approach of the period when the great mass of American labor shall not find its employment in the field; when the young men of the country shall be obliged to shut their eyes upon external nature, upon the heavens and the earth, and immerse themselves in close and unwholesome workshops;

when they shall be obliged to shut their ears to the
bleating of their own flocks upon their own hills, and
to the voice of the lark that cheers them at their
plows, that they may open them in dust and smoke and
steam to the perpetual whirl of spools and spindles,
and the grating of rasps and saws." [1]

Were evidence needed that nature gains a hold upon
the common heart, it would be enough to point to the
universal resort to the country when those who dwell
in cities have a holiday. The love of hunting and
fishing is chiefly a disguised fondness for nature, which
unromantic men do not like to confess. The annual
hegira from the cities shows how the love of the
country abides, and the healing of the ravages of city
life under the summer's gentle ministry proves the
power of the rural environment. It reaches all sorts
and conditions of men, and it is not without notable
effects as it lays hold of inferior persons. It is precisely this refining and stimulating influence that the
plain people remaining in the country require.

There are two modes in which this pervasive and
potent influence acts with heightened power. The
first in importance, as in time, is through the poetic
tradition,—the poetic tradition rather than poetry.
The reason for the distinction is that it is not necessary
to read what the poets have written to profit by that
richer environment which belongs to the country in
consequence of poetry. By a subtle potency the rural
environment comes to be not the obtrusive masses of

[1] On the Repeal of the Embargo, March, 1814, quoted from
McMaster's " Daniel Webster," p. 86.

earth, nor the monotonous acres of grass, nor the
dazzling stretch of endless flowers, nor the disturbing
chatter of the birds; but instead of these, hills that
speak of freedom, a sky that brings the infinite near,
meadows verdant with beauty, air vocal with song.
Beauty, sublimity, music, freedom, are in the soul.
Whence came they? It is a habit of souls. It is the
way of men. It is something that has come to be in
the course of the generations. It is the spiritual
environment of the race. The poets are at once the
creators and the expression of this world of feeling;
because they have sung, it is, and because it is, they
have sung.

Literature supplies speech so that every mood of
nature becomes intelligible and every mood of man is
articulate. When a rich literature is the inheritance
of a people, the environment is no longer dumb; it is
living and vocal and personal. Cloud-shadowed
mountain and murmuring stream and wind-kissed
flower speak messages of that ideal country into
which every poet makes an " Excursion." Few
country folk may read what the poets have written,
yet the tradition of higher meanings lives. As men
who never open the Bible are trained under its
spiritual illumination, which has become an atmosphere of the mind, so the people that possess a literature receive an exaltation from it, even if the eye is
unused to follow lines of print. Literature is a spirit
before it is a page of type, and there is a telepathy
which passes on the inspiration regardless of eye and
ear. If one chooses to add that not every one is sen-

sitive to such high communication, it is quite true; but
the tendency of the time is to make common what has
been the felicity of the rarest souls.

The other mode in which the influence of nature is
felt is just now in high favor. Nature study is opening the eyes to a myriad beauties and meanings of the
world.   There is a wealth of beauty in natural objects
—the fast accumulating mental capital of the race.
Nature study stands for a middle section of the new
knowledge, lying between the poetic tradition and technical science.   It is more exact than poetry, freer than
science.   It is a stream in the valley between these
two uplands, with many tributaries from either side.
It affords choice material for education ; it should be a
lifelong enrichment.

The first dividend from nature study is a peculiar
pleasure in knowing the names of birds and trees and
flowers,—as if the name bore the burden of human
interest and told the secret of companionship with
many generations of men.   " Naming things," says a
true lover of nature, " is one of the oldest and simplest
of human pastimes.   Children play at it with their
dolls and toy animals.   In fact, it was the first game
ever played on earth, for the Creator who planted the
garden eastward knew well what would please the
childish heart of man when he brought all the new-
made creatures to Adam, to see what he would call
them." [1]   If we cannot play the Edenic game of giving
names, it pleases quite as well to call each object of

[1] Henry Van Dyke, " Little Rivers, At the Sign of the Balsam
Bough."

interest and beauty by its accepted name,—thus establishing an acquaintance soon ripening into intimacy. Enthusiastic lovers of animals even recognize and name individuals. After reading the chapter telling the story of the friendly bird, one likes the dedication of " Wilderness Ways " :

> " To Kilooleet, Little Sweet-
> Voice, who shares my camp and
> Makes sunshine as I work and play."

But names mean far more when the life-story is told. The true nature teacher tells the tale of hoarded soil, and seed-wafting winds, and dripping clouds, and stamps on memory a picture of the flower in its surroundings and groupings. The result is acquaintance with the living world rather than items of knowledge illustrated in herbariums—those old catacombs of education. Thus a modern teacher writes of an excursion with young children :

" So it was a great and momentous day when we set out for River Forest. All had agreed to gather no flowers where it would spoil a picture, and because the teacher knew where the most beautiful pictures were, all were to keep close to her. The first picture was a colony of several hepaticas on the side of the terrace leading down into the basin. We noted the open blossoms, the nodding buds, the soft furry covering of the buds and young leaves, and the rich purple tones of the old ones. We looked and looked and closed our eyes and looked again. Then we went on to the great host of spring-beauties camping on the plain. Later, we tarried by a mass of purple phlox at the foot of a linden-tree. The morning's work consisted in fixing these three pictures and a fourth which was the landscape, the general setting for them all, the old flood-plain with its magnificent elms and white maples then in blossom, the broad blue river on one side, the terrace on the other, and the sunshine over all.

"Each then selected a single flower to take home as a souvenir and we hurried to the train. The children were perfectly satisfied with their one blossom ; the beautiful scene was left unmarred, and to this day those little folks can close their eyes and see their four River Forest pictures. Had they gathered the flowers, their interest would have centred on that, the picture remaining would have been confused, and the final memory that of the faded flowers in their little hot hands. But the flowers that they really brought home are—dare we say ?—immortal." [1]

It should not be forgotten that before the wonders of nature are in the books, they are on the hillside, and on the river bank, and in the woodland. The writer from whom the preceding paragraphs are taken recalls appreciatively a wistful young teacher attending a summer school who told her of happy children spending recesses with polliwogs and minnows at the brook, and stealing into the schoolhouse at an early hour to catch the house-wren on her nest on the stove-pipe—and then expressed her regret that she had neither time nor means for nature study.

[1] Mary P. Anderson, "The Protection of Our Native Plants," in the *Journal of the New York Botanical Garden*, Vol. V, pp. 76, 77.

The school garden supplies abundant materials for these studies. Whenever introduced it fascinates the children, applies their knowledge, opens to them the world of nature, interests them in agriculture, informs them in their life work, develops their taste, and assures the beautifying of their future homes. Almost universal in Europe, school gardens are becoming common in America, where desolate school-yards vividly reveal the need.[1]

Nature study cannot be pressed too fast in the rural schools. It promises the one thing needful for the uplifting influence of nature upon those who dwell with her. More than anything else it will make the boys and girls contented in their country homes. There comes to my mind the memory of a young man, to whom few years were given on earth. Beyond all whom I have known he loved the woods and fields, the brook that loitered by his home, and the river that edged the meadows with silver. He knew all living things; his ear caught and interpreted every sound; his eye saw pictures in all fragments of nature. Scientist without learning, poet without speech, he was the untaught example of the ideal now sought in the schools. Nature's child, his life was full of quiet joy, of content, and peace.

---

[1] For the best brief account of this new form of education see Circulars of Educational Information, No. XIII, issued by the Department of Education of Vermont, where may be found "School Gardens" by Edith Goodyear Alger. The Board of Agriculture of Massachusetts has published a series of pamphlets which are excellent guides in many lines of nature study.

There is a hint for younger persons in the experience of a man not too old to learn in his ninety-fourth year. " I have just noticed," he said, " that the dandelion opens more than once. Watching it has interested me, and I am sorry I have missed so much all these years." The need in rural life is this power of vision. When it is developed so that every fence-corner is a bit of wonderland, and every web hung by the wayside excites a deeper interest than all Nebuchadnezzar's hanging gardens, and each up-turned rock suggests an earlier world of seas and lands and outbreaking fires, then will nature seem to be not so much a coy spirit for shy and difficult intercourse as a counsellor of infinite experience, a companion ripe with wisdom, and ever ready with strange and fascinating tales.

This elementary and practical science need not take the place of those literary studies that open up the world in a different way. Both enlargements of knowledge are required. Certainly the untrained rustic who knows nothing beyond loving his rural scenes with primal affection needs for the enrichment of his life what literature and science can bestow. When to the rural environment of material forms are added soul from poetry and rational interest from science, there will be in the impact of nature upon the country people a stimulus and an influence that will open all the faculties of the mind, let loose all the streams of life in the heart, and develop character that will be strong, righteous, beautiful. If this seems a too ideal view, it is warranted, in part, by what history relates of the power of nature over a people, as in Greece, Italy, Switzerland, New England, and in part also, by the hope of a new education, certain to come with untold blessing. There is a subtle sympathy between high moods of the soul and the quietness, sublimity, and beauty of nature.

> " The universal forms
> Of human nature, in a spot like this,
> Present themselves to all men's view." [1]

This chapter began by disclaiming that the influences it presents are new; they are, in fact, as old as the occupancy of the earth by man. They have been seasoned in all climates, and they have had part in molding many races. Out of the old, however, is born the new. There is an Old Testament of nature which is being superseded by a new gospel. Fear has given place to love; severe obedience has learned the eager confidence of faith. The attitude towards the material world has changed. It is no longer conceived as spared from divine wrath for a brief day before cleansing fires, but as expressing in beautiful evolutions the thoughts of God, having passed through creative fires and having the promise of endurance beyond human ken. Now is the propitious moment for a new education. The environment depends upon the mind. We cannot say with enthusiastic idealists that every man may create new heavens and a new earth; but it is no extravagance to believe that every instructed child may see a world and live joyfully in a

[1] Wordsworth, " The Excursion," Book Eighth.

world unknown in former times. The beautiful tradition of literature is accessible as never before through the multiplication of libraries and the cheapness of books. If all be done that the time invites, a new environment will form new men and new women, though they dwell in houses built by their fathers and till the fields on which their predecessors toiled.

CHAPTER XII

PERSONAL FORCES

BOSWELL relates that Dr. Johnson once refused a living of considerable value in Lincolnshire. The thought of Dr. Johnson in a country parish seems not to have aroused any sense of humor in the faithful biographer, who after mentioning the conscientious convictions of his master concerning his personal duty, adds the pertinent consideration that Dr. Johnson's "love of London life was so strong, that he would have felt himself an exile in any other place, particularly if residing in the country."[1] It would be the height of folly to deny the attraction of the city. The mere mention of men of the type of Johnson and Macaulay is enough to make it plain that the city is the proper setting for thinkers and men of affairs when they reach the cosmopolitan size.

It is interesting, however, to find Dr. Johnson oppressed with the size of the little London of his day. Boswell had remarked, as they walked to church on Good Friday "that one disadvantage arising from the immensity of London was, that nobody was heeded by his neighbor; there was no fear of censure for not observing Good Friday, as it ought to be kept, and as it is kept in country towns." The doctor contended

[1] "The Life of Samuel Johnson," Vol. I, Chap. IX.

that, upon the whole, the day was very well observed even in London. " He, however, owned," writes Boswell, " that London was too large." [1]   The philosopher added more to the effect that it was not a case of the head outgrowing the body—a thing tolerable enough in his opinion, no doubt—but of a development in which head and body could not be made out at all. Evidently there would be some hazard if this critical old lover were to see his beloved London to-day.   The gigantic city, however, has no lack of enchantments for those whose tastes have changed with the times. The present passion is for bigness, and cities seem never too large.   Not only with ardent lovers but with wise men the country town is out of favor,—a little David out in the field while the big brothers pass before Samuel.

The love of the city can give a good account of itself.   There meet the great currents of the world— whether of trade, of government, or of thought.   To dwell in the midst of great affairs is stimulating and wholesome.   The throng of men has a fascination ; the crowd is exhilarating.   The sense of a living touch as one meets his fellows elbow to elbow is more human and social than the craving for solitudes. These personal influences, attracting to the city, must be added to the industrial forces that drive men thither.   This aspect of the problem is well stated by a suggestive writer upon rural life a generation ago. " If you ask these people," says Mr. Eggleston, " why they are so eager for the town, and so ready to leave

[1] Op. Cit., Vol. II, Chap. XI.

the country, their answer when you fairly get it is,
'The country is dull.' . . . It is the defective social
element of our country life which is the most efficient
cause of the depletion of the country and the disproportionate gathering of population in the large
towns and cities."[1] A more philosophical observer,
writing from the English standpoint, confirms this
judgment. Mr. Lecky writes: "But every one who
has much practical acquaintance with country life will,
I believe, agree that the movement (migration of the
agricultural population to the great towns) has been
greatly intensified by the growing desire for more ex-
citement and amusement."[2] This, doubtless, is a true
view, and we need not dissent even when this increasing restlessness is attributed to education. Instead of
finding fault with those who are discontented in the
country, we do better to recognize in their desire for
the city an expansion of mind and an inevitable phase
of human experience in the advance of civilization.

It is well to sound the matter to the bottom and
find in the centripetal social tendency an instinct developed in the evolutionary process. Natural selection
early set its mark upon gregariousness, for during long
eras of desolating war those who dwelt apart perished.
A home upon the farm itself is the recent boon of
peace and national stability; the village and the city
have been places of refuge. The result of sifting the
race for ages under this principle is the evolution of

---

[1] Nathaniel Hillyer Eggleston, "Villages and Village Life," pp. 32,
37.

[2] "Democracy and Liberty," Vol. I, p. 319. Cf. Vol. II, p. 477.

an instinct villageward and cityward. The village loafer, rightly understood, simply squares himself with the forces that have made mankind, and offers no further protest against this social gravitation. And this same hunger for comradeship drives the uprooted migrant far beyond the neighboring village to the never-filled cities. To stay apart, to work alone, to live in seclusion, may have great compensations; but to speak of them is scarcely more effective than to reason with the avalanche concerning the glory of the mountain after it has felt the joy of yielding to the forces that have pulled at its heart since the world began.

The concession of the supreme attraction of the city and the recognition of the centripetal impulse in its full force—as if social gravitation varied with the mass—need not obscure those personal influences that enrich and mold rural life. Along the roadsides and in the villages life goes on with all its wide and deep human interests. There is rich profiting from such personal contacts as the country affords. In the development of men the personal environment must ever have chief significance; its unique features in city or country must be traced with care. Of these personal forces of the rural environment—rich influences even for a scattered people—our study must now take note if it is to fathom what is taking place.

Environment suggests to many minds only soil, climate, formations of land and sea; more important by far are the social tradition, literature, institutions, men. Here we speak of groups of men into which the individual is born. It matters much whether one first sees the light in the midst of farmers and villagers, or in the huge conglomeration of the city. The theme is a composite one, and it is not easy to keep its elements apart. On the one hand the rural condition—chiefly the paucity of men—favors character of peculiar types ; and on the other hand these men in their turn become an influence modifying and enriching the lives of their neighbors. The essential facts will come into view if we consider first the room and freedom and afterwards the closeness of personal contact in the country.

Originality requires chiefly to be let alone, and there is not much to say of the first topic beyond the recognition of the negative influence of the rural environment,—if mere vacuity and spaciousness can be called influences. The country protects from fads and crazes —the excesses of the imitative instinct. The more common putting of it is that the country is free from the temptations of which the city is full. A temptation is chiefly a bad example that appeals to the imitative instinct. In these times when social life is highly developed,—when a multitude of people do the same things, talk of the same things, read the same things, —we have something different from temptation in the old sense. There is an assault of society upon the individual with no sense of a moral issue to arouse resistance. The tendency is for vast masses to become passive to the sentiment or superstition or delirium of the hour. As these social storms pass over, they give an agreeable variety to the mental weather ; many days with no air stirring are hardly to be endured. These pleasant excitements develop an unhealthful dependence and a feverish condition. Country people may be ignorant of ephemeral agitations to their great profit. Movements of real significance will reach them, but fads of the hour will not play havoc with their originality. Isolation is so far a desirable protection.

It should be repeated here, also, that natural selection now spares a richer variety of human life and character in the country. Partly by the discipline of common excitements but more by the crushing of exceptional individuals, the city tends to develop a single type; other kinds cannot get on. In the country it is not necessary to get on; it is enough to subsist. The result is that queer and freaky types are found in the country, and also superior kinds of folk not adapted to a commercial civilization. Not all the music of human life can be played on the commercial octave. Novelists go to the country for character, which they may often put through the discipline of life in the city. In the country there is more hope of coming upon those men and women of the highest charm, who can step from hillside and valley and quiet street into the bright world of dreams with the least lightening of their footfall and the slightest change in mien and manner. Or is it a trick of the trade to seek in some remote and unvisited spot types that are not found in the streets where books are printed, as the classic poets peopled distant coasts with Sirens and Cyclops although they well knew that such interesting

personal variants were never seen within the range of
actual voyages? Be that as it may, the theory of
natural selection is now in conspiracy with poetry to
populate places where life is less strenuous with a
diversity of human sorts, ranging from the quaint and
grotesque to the guileless and fragile in every degree
of refinement. The survival of these perishable types
is due to a more catholic action of selection in the
country; but what happens to individuals while they
live—the free unfolding of their idiosyncracies—must
be treated as part of the influence of the friendly and
roomy rural environment. It is not in the country
that we have occasion for Dr. Johnson's remark,
" Commerce has left the people no singularities."

And here one welcomes the generous provision for
an agreeable variety of mankind in the mutation
theory of evolution.[1] De Vries has given scientific
standing to Professor William James's rash accounting
for great men by the seeming accidents of the germ
mixtures and tiltings.[2] How else can genius be explained than as a sudden mutation in the human
species? Why at the middle of the last century
was Boston distinguished by men of genius, whom
the whole world recognized? And why is there no
apostolic succession in poetry and eloquence and
statesmanship? If there is a " cycle of law,"—
now inviting investigation although pronounced by
Professor James " so remotely connected with the

[1] Cf. p. 172.
[2] " Great Men, Great Thoughts, and the Environment," an acute
and charming article in the *Atlantic Monthly* for October, 1880.

order which science observes that we have nothing to do with it,"—in whose mysterious determinations genius is thrust into the world as an apparent sport of a shifting species, we may expect to come upon many sorts of men—quaint and queer, eccentric and dowered with genius—wherever new "mixtures and tiltings" appear. These interesting persons will be born in country and city, but we may conjecture that the instability of the human species will be greatest in the country.

But our theme requires us to go no further than to say that originality is less likely to be repressed in rural communities. The crust of convention is thickest in the city, and is not so easily rent by the fires of genius. This individual spontaneity is precious beyond all valuation. Its significance is seen best in literature which is great in the degree in which it expresses individual feeling and conviction. Hawthorne and Emerson are placed by general consent at the head of American men of letters; both are supremely original. Hawthorne brooded, indeed, over the New England tradition; but he brought to it the flaming Sinai of his own soul, and his solemn and beautiful rendering of it abides in the tone of our spiritual landscape. Emerson was far less reverent; "serene insolence" is Professor Wendell's phrase for his attitude.[1] These men have made their mood felt far beyond Longfellow, rich in the traffic of cultures; or Lowell, spoilsman of learning and true knight of reform. Whitman alone has kindred originality, but his mood

[1] Barrett Wendell, "A Literary History of America," p. 313.

was too personal and too alien to beauty to become the mental atmosphere of a people. To claim for the country any of these citizens of the world would be childish, although the two greatest names are forever associated with a quiet village; the point is rather that the characteristic of the highest genius is an original and inevitable spontaneity—an intensity of individuality that is uncompromising and dominating. Our interest is in milder distillations of this spirit which enrich the variety of men. The possibility that genius may appear among these variants gives additional zest. Professor Giddings by another line of approach reaches with assurance the conclusion which is here only suggested as probable. " Genius," he says, " is rarely born in the town. The world's great faiths have germinated in the desert among mountain heights. Its great policies have been suggested by unsophisticated men. It owes its great discoveries and its immortal creations to those who have lived with nature and with simple folk." His view is that the country produces original ideas—the raw materials of social life, and that the city combines ideas and forms the social mind.[1]

Turning now to the environment which receives into itself this wealth of individuality, there are features of the way in which country people live together that are significant. The variety being so rich and the quality sometimes being so fine, there is endless fascination in one's neighbors. The country has developed two unique forms of social intercourse, of which many

[1] " The Principles of Sociology," p. 347.

biting things have been said with doubtful wisdom—
the habit of gossip and the nightly conclave in store
or post-office. This gossip is not often malicious; in
fact it grows out of the interest of the people in one
another. It should be remembered that in the country neighborly intercourse ripens for decades; that acquaintance is an ancestral tradition; and that family
friendships are an inheritance. It easily follows that a
roof cannot be shingled; nor a field be sown; nor a
child sent to school; nor a courtship advanced on its
intricate way, without the attention of the neighborhood. On the whole this is a harmless exercise of
friendliness, and the exasperation at it is a somewhat
petty indignation over small affairs. But that group
about the stove assembling nightly—what can be said
of that? Chiefly that the men concerned enjoy their
evenings. When it is considered what a deal of trouble
the urban citizen takes with his theatre and his club,
the marvel is that so much can be had at so cheap a
rate. This pleasure depends upon the variety of character. There must be a wise man for an oracle, a
witty man for jokes, a story-teller to keep things going,
and dumb associates to listen and laugh. This is a
social ideal whose equal is not to be found in social
devices made to order. To have some one to talk to
is felicity on the one side, and to hear talk meets a
need on the other. This is at once a school of politics
and an exchange for the wisdom of life. All that is
needed is a Plato to make an Academy or an Aristotle
for a Lyceum. Though Platos and Aristotles are not
numerous, there are men in plenty who know a thou-

sand things that would open the eyes of those wise old Greeks. This is an institution to be reckoned with, for it controls public sentiment and gives wings to opinion. The foundation of its success is its spontaneity, the variety of character, and the pleasure varying sorts of men have in each other.

This delightful social intercourse has a more serious aspect. Could the best people be retained in the country, the variety of character would leave little to be desired. The pessimist has failed to see the strength of his case when he stops short with his alarm over natural selection; more important is the loss out of the environment which molds character. The inspiration of a half dozen families, their vicarious experiments in the application of new knowledge, their modernized farming, their taste and skill in living, their social leadership, their public counsel and influence, may easily lift a whole community to a high level. When the best emigrate the loss is incalculable, and to one who appreciates the rôle of imitation in social development it seems remediless. The best that can be said is that the people who stay in the old homes are not to be disparaged. It is easy to think of mutual corruption and of social depravity as worthless people meet and contaminate one another, but human stuff is not so decadent as this. A more penetrating vision discovers a vast wholesomeness even in depleted rural communities, and much of the human material which comes into being with a pristine freshness in the country is immune to the diffused moral infection. In the average country town to-day the personal environment is such that boys and girls born into it need not be commiserated.

Much of what passes for social communication in the city is defective. One is never more isolated than in a crowd in which no face is familiar. There is a flood of experience of humanity in the abstract, but it is not much more serviceable than the philosopher's meditation upon the universal man. Indeed so far as actual contact is concerned, one might as well be in the human section of Plato's dim region of ideas as on Broadway. People, people everywhere, but not a soul to know! We fall back upon pure metaphysics and face the unknowable crowd in despair. This overwhelming sense of humanity in hordes is not acquaintance, and this is one reason why the city, which seems to be society at its height, is the place where men hide from one another and go their independent way. In the country all the people have some knowledge of everybody within the area of the common life, and nearer neighbors live in the intimacy that dates, it may be, from the friendship of their grandfathers.

To be known is an immense moral help. Boswell was quite right in regretting the absence of censure in the city. Men escape it because they are lost in the crowd. Nothing is more demoralizing than the consciousness that one may do what he pleases without observation. Young men are peculiarly exposed when they first take up their residence in cities. In the old home they were restrained by the desire for the good opinion of those who would note every lapse and record every excess in their book of judgment. When there is no longer a book of judgment, the strain upon moral purpose is acute. It is a question whether being known or knowing others has greater social value, but both are at their best in the country.

In the city the separation of classes makes a bad condition worse. Foreign populations herd together, gaining a richer contact within the nationality but setting back the process of assimilation by decades. Fortunate is the immigrant who finds himself in the midst of a rural population. He is quickly known and appreciated at his just worth, and he speedily knows those whose imitation is for him the way of progress. His racial peculiarities are soluble in such conditions, whereas the huge masses of alien life in the city are scarcely open to percolating streams. Comprehensive forces like education and factory discipline are most effective in the city, but personal contact is peculiarly close and powerful in the country.

One simple rural condition has passed without notice, although its consequences are greater than can be conceived. The hired man is in closest association with the family; he works by the side of his employer; he sits at the common table; he is the companion of the children. Coming as a raw immigrant, he may remain until he appropriates the mode of farming, the style of living, the standard of character, and even the religion of a higher civilization. This is a social settlement reversed; instead of a family thrust into an inferior population, the inferior person is put into the family. By such methods as these Nature takes care of her children and steals a march on the social reformer.

The human product of the city has never been more accurately described than by Mr. Pearson, who believes that town work is on the average less educative than country work, but that town life turns the scale.[1] When he sketches the city man, however, the picture is not altogether reassuring. He is shrewd, alert, versatile, quicker and more resourceful than the countryman. These qualities, it will be noted, are egoistic rather than altruistic. It is as if city life lacked a certain sense of personal values,—as if a man were to be measured for wrestling, to be outwitted, to be used. Such would seem to be the inevitable attitude of those who meet human multitudes—mere abstract mankind, unknown, unloved—and wrest out of the mass the advance of their own fortune, as they might mine coal. Shrewdness, craft, versatility are necessary and honorable qualities, but they are the device of a competing weakness rather than the exercise of a masterful competence. The countryman is helpless in the city until he has profited by a new training, but in his own less exacting environment he is equal to the situation and can be brotherly. " There is not," writes the man who of all in his time has had the richest experience of great and small social groups,—" there is not in the cities the same sense of common, underlying brotherhood which there is still in country districts."[2]

[1] Charles H. Pearson, " National Life and Character," p. 338. Cf. p 159.
[2] President Theodore Roosevelt, in *The Outlook*, August 30, 1902.

The country fosters individuality, variety, independence ; but when these products of a somewhat solitary life reach the strength that threatens social fitness, they are directed to a new issue in brotherhood by close and pleasant association in the neighborhood and in the town, in which every one knows his fellows and is known by them. This brotherhood is easier because the rural ideal, at its best, is to enjoy simple and common things rather than to possess rich and divisive things. The great sources of happiness cannot be owned and monopolized. No man can survey the blue of heaven and stake out his claim there. No court will convict of trespass the beauty-loving eye that pays no heed to title deeds. There are no trusts to grind the poor in friendship or virtue. The primal personal relationships, therefore, are thwarted less in the country, and the native warmth of heart, not cooled by convention and competition, has its way.

An inexhaustible variety of persons in intimate association, subject to slight temptation to exploit one another but disposed rather to enjoy the riches of fellowship that increase with the using, is an influential part of that environment which perpetually acts upon the country people, who in spite of every wasting and demoralizing force are the surprise of our modern civilization.

CHAPTER XIII

NEW FACTORS

In the opening chapters of Marius the Epicurean, Walter Pater presents a half ruined farm-villa as the refuge of all that was most beautiful in the old Roman world. A rich tradition is the possession of the country long after the city has welcomed novelties from all regions of the earth. Paganism—the religion of the villages—is a verbal witness to this rural conservatism. How pleasantly the scent of the bean-fields mingles with the cloud of incense! how perfectly those wreaths of flowers suit the instruments of labor, as masters and servants go together in solemn procession along the dry paths of vineyard and corn-field! how intimately near are the cultivation of the earth and the care of the flocks to the elementary conditions of life in which primitive religion and primitive morals emerge! how this farm life deriving grace from the culture of the olive and the vine contributes an ideal dignity to character! how impossible is vulgarity in a place so full of venerable memories. As this magician weaves his witcheries, the reader forgets whether he is in a real Italy of the Antonines, or where Keats on the sides of Latmus assembles his shepherds,

" Such as sat listening round Apollo's pipe."

These stirring times have scant reverence for the old
ideals; even those quiet places which are the proper
haunt of venerable tradition have bowed to the reno-
vation. The new world is the environment of men
everywhere, and farm and village cannot escape the
transformation. The country people, as all others, are
developing new elements and types of character as
they make the adjustment to the new environment.
It is an unfavorable hour to appraise rural life when it
has lost the old sanity and fitness, and has not won the
new symmetry and adaptation. In this it shares the
misfortune of the age whose tumultuous energies excite
the sympathetic Whitman to an utterance as strange
in poetry as modern life is new to the world. And
yet ideal elements are in this rebuilding of the Titans,
as Kipling has taught us in his eager appreciation of
the day's work in all latitudes. If we have lost Apollo,
Vulcan, at least, remains.

The new thing in the rural environment is the world
itself. Once the environment of the farm was the
neighborhood; the environment of the village was the
encircling farms and the local tradition. This statement must be amended, of course, to admit the
influence of national ideals, of world literatures, of
catholic religious faiths. That men were inadequately
reached by these powers that knit up the common
brotherhood, appears in the violence of the contro-
versial spirit. There was little travel; no daily newspaper brought tidings from the ends of the earth; few
conventions assembled for discussion and common
action; educational centres did not radiate the shock

of a new intellectual life to every hamlet; federations and unions did not bind men, near and remote, into the fellowship that makes one composite type of many human sorts. It was an age of sects, intolerant from lack of acquaintance. The simplicity of life, and the uniformity of conditions, and the supremacy of a few ideals alone prevented the disruption of society. All this is changed. The country town is now linked to the great world by the railway; by telegraph and telephone; by a daily mail delivered at every door, or in every neighborhood; [1] by newspapers diffusing over every hillside the items of knowledge that inform the residents of cities; by interest in college athletics, and the national game, and whatever is the talk of the moment; by orders and societies of many kinds; by the developing life of the nation, already threatening local democracy by its swift advance towards imperial- ism; by the softening of religious asperities and the tendency to merge religious organizations.

The most vital contacts with the larger world—most vital because inevitable—are in the industrial sphere. The country town of to-day produces for the world, and it obtains its supplies from the commerce of the world. This is at once a cause of weakness and a

---

[1] " At the beginning of the fiscal year, 1899, there were about 200 routes in operation. There are now more than 25,000 routes, bring- ing a daily mail service to more than 12,000,000 of our people in rural communities, enlarging the circulation of the newspaper and the mag- azine, increasing communication, and relieving the isolation of life on the farm."—Hon. Elihu Root, Address as Temporary Chairman of the National Republican Convention, June 21, 1904.

source of strength. As the thumb has lost its deftness for the work of a finger, and has grown stiff and awkward by its habit of meeting the fingers in the grasp in which all work together, so the country town is no longer able to care for itself, but being essential to the society of which it is a part shares in the growing prosperity and power of all. The rural population, as a whole, cannot fall into decay,—as readily may the thumb dwindle while the hand has full exercise. Fears for the country people are needless. The growth of the city compels the prosperity of the country. The form of country life may change, but ready and successful change is a sign of health.

Our present concern is with the effects upon character of the new adjustment to the economic order. Are the country people to be better or worse after they have achieved this adaptation? With or against their will they must produce for the world and receive from the world a fair compensation in the products of its labor. The question is whether these persons, taking their place in the world system, will be of a higher or a lower character than their predecessors, who lived the independent life of the isolated community

On the optimistic side of this question is our instinctive faith in the wholesomeness of great relations. It exalts man to make him a part of a world system. The consciousness of ministry gives dignity and the sense of value, without which life tends to lose heart. Higher intelligence is required for the operation of a world system than for local independence. The significance of the immense development of technical education is found here. Somewhere in the system all that is known of science must be applied, and there must be men trained in this high intelligence. The world system was not possible until the advance of knowledge brought those inventions and discoveries through which the industrial system has been wrought out. But the social is more important than the mechanical engineer. The industrial system is oftener imperiled by moral than by intellectual unfitness. The supreme question is whether the men now dominating the world have moral character of such trustworthiness, justice, and generosity that the present scale of cöoperation and organization can be maintained. One need not hesitate to say that the demand far exceeds the ability of any previous generation. It may be freely granted that there are alarming betrayals of trust and disheartening examples of unsocial men in places of high social responsibility; but on the other hand the industrial task of the present age would be as overwhelming to the slender moral equipment of earlier times, as it would be staggering to their intelligence. The ascetic virtue, the other-worldliness, the unsympathetic justice of the Puritan could make no headway in modern life. Great ideals of service, mighty impulses of brotherhood, acute sympathy with other lives, high conceptions of the common good, are essential to a world system,—these are coming under the compulsion of the new environment. Because they have not fully possessed the minds of men, disorder breaks out, and we are ever on the brink of social collapse. Any profound interpretation of the modern world, however, is bound to find in it an amazing ethical advance.

The effect of world changes in general must be distinguished from the effect upon individuals. The demand for these high qualities of intelligence and morality is not evenly distributed. The farmer need not understand the applications of electricity; it is enough if experts are competent to provide the electrical equipment. The vicarious principle has a great field in the intellectual world, for a few men possess the knowledge in which society prospers. It is not so clear that the altruistic temper—important as it is for administrators of large affairs—can be supplied by a few men. The superior morality demanded by the modern system must be diffused throughout all ranks and classes; so intricate are the moral reciprocities that an inactive partner cannot draw dividends in ethics as in science. Superior leaders often go before the people, but the people must follow. Oftener still a superior people forces an able and high-minded leadership. There must always be a close correspondence between the masses and the leaders. If we have selfish monopoly, the spirit of monopoly is in the hearts of the people. If we have captains of industry who count the lives of other men as material to be consumed, these men who are sacrificed would be equally indifferent to the claims of others if they were in the place of power. The selfishness of capital is exactly matched by the selfishness of labor; and every generosity of administration is rivalled by the disinterestedness of the workers. When the leaders are ready for a moral advance, the people keep pace with them ; and when the masses come to a right mind, right-minded administrators appear. First or last there is one character from top to bottom, from centre to circumference of society. The great debate whether evolution is through leaders or though masses will never end, for both methods have conspicuous illustration; but the truth that should be equally evident to all disputants is that the morality demanded for the social life must be diffused throughout the social organism.

There will be, therefore, one standard of commercial and industrial morality in the great offices and on the remote farms. Sometimes the influence will be from above downward; again that which first exists beneath will rise to the top. A moral force of incalculable power, penetrating all communities, touching all lives, radiates from the great industrial centres. On the great scale fraud is impossible permanently. In the actual production and sale of goods it is demonstrated to the satisfaction of all men that honest and fair dealing is the only practical basis for business. The sudden development of the corporation in an unsettled time, when even full publicity would not eliminate the element of hazard, has dazzled astute men into a momentary blindness, so that they do not see the absurdity of conducting the largest transactions without regard to the demands of morality. This commercial criminality cannot last, and temporary aberrations of those who exploit conjecture, and capitalize contingent

opportunities, and buy and sell delusions, disturb, but
cannot arrest the growing influence of great enterprises
in behalf of a high morality. Things bought and sold
must be as represented. This elementary truth is so
far demonstrated that trust is the common attitude of
men of business,—suspicion being retained only as a
safeguard against those who do not know or refuse to
follow the rules of the game. The old higgling over
prices, asking one price and expecting another, has
passed away for the most part. Petty deceptions are
now regarded as indications of a mean spirit. Mere
sharpness is at a discount. Certain rural characteristics once common are fading out, just as financial
chicanery is being swiftly replaced by expert administration in railway presidencies. Sinuosities, petty or
colossal, are already under impartial condemnation and
—what may prove quite as effective—under universal
contempt. Whatever of high morality emerges from
the conflicts of the time, becomes the standard and example for all the people. Every country boy grows
up with ideas of dealing with his fellow men, that prevail in high places, for these count far more in his eyes
than the actual practice of his rustic neighbors. Our
conclusion then must be that the faith in the wholesomeness of even a lowly participation in great affairs
is not altogether rash. There is something more than
contact with bigness; there is the vital communion
through which the most precious elements of character
are disseminated.

It is often forgotten that the materialism of the present day is most wonderfully allied to ethics. What

we see is not so much a new material development as a new embodiment of the moral life. Never has the world seen such an environment for the production of the noblest character as that which now presses upon men in every part of the great workshop in the midst of whose din they live. In the case of the country people the struggle for adaptation means the remaking of character. The indolent, passive, meditative, vegetative man must give place to the alert, virile, strenuous man.

Economic adjustment may be won in either of two ways. On the one hand a man may lower the price of his product by lessening the expenditure upon himself. This low-cost laborer is everywhere; he appears in every vacant place, abhorring a vacuum like the air. He is in the country as well as the city. One great movement in the country is the effort to meet the demands of the situation by cheapening men. This is the significance of the displacement of the old stock by the immigrant, upon which we have commented elsewhere. But there is another and a better way of making the required adjustment; it is possible to meet the exactions of the market by new thrift, by better management, and by higher intelligence. The farmer must do the one thing or the other; he must be a better farmer or an inferior man. The downward tendency will have a limited field; in the main the new adaptation will be won by a higher intelligence. This means an uplifting of great masses of the country people, and for this process the instrumentalities are at hand.

The new agricultural education is to do for farming what technical education has done for manufactures and transportation. But there will be one striking difference! In manufactures many workmen may be employed who know only the part of the work that falls to them in the division of labor; on the farm there can be no such distribution. The agricultural college may introduce methods, certify facts, conduct experiments, with large benefits to those who have no comprehension of scientific processes. New applications of chemistry promise as great changes in farming as have been wrought by mechanical invention. Though the farmer need not be a chemist to profit by the advance of agricultural chemistry, and though he may be a beneficiary of scientific progress of whose technicalities he knows nothing, he must have a high intellectual development in more general ways to avail himself of the improvements offered him by the learned members of his profession. There is still a deplorable stubbornness in many rural communities in following the lead of the agricultural colleges; this will not disappear until the small and hostile mind of ignorance is succeeded by the large and open mind of intelligence. Meanwhile those who refuse the development by which they might become competent for their task will dwindle to that cheap and meagre manhood which is the baneful alternative in the present stress of competition.

The department of agriculture of the national government, and the agricultural colleges and experiment stations of the states are fast appropriating the results of science for the farmer. The treatment of soils, the breeding of stock, the feeding of animals, the suppression of contagious and infectious diseases, the destruction of injurious insects, the making of butter and cheese, the production of plants and flowers, the adaptation of seed to soil and climate, involve scientific factors to an unappreciated degree. The new agriculture will apply these triumphs of knowledge. Whether this is done by trained men, or by men of open and thrifty mind for the new authoritative tradition, there is here a sublime hope; the world that exacts for its markets will supply those upon whom it lays its compulsion with its sciences. To be a part of so generous a world means much for character and for largeness of life and attainment.

One thing more must be named in this strange new materialism. We look for sordid elements, and we find a new ethics and a vast enrichment of the intellect. After the same generous fashion this commerce which is feared fills the home with refinement and exalts taste. The time when the farmer need be known by his dress or his manners has passed. His home need not be provincial. The adapted farmer will be a large consumer; only thus can he play his part in his reciprocity with the world, and discharge his full obligation towards the urban population. Hence the cheap immigrant, reducing living to its lowest terms, is not a permanent solution of the rural problem. Country life, relieved of its solitude by steam train and trolley, by telephone and free delivery of mails, with electric lights in villages and on farms, with electric power added to countless mechanical devices, with furnishings such as the taste of the time approves, with books and periodicals and music, with large leisure won as drudgery is laid off, will yet turn the scale and outdo the city in attractions for many persons of simple and refined tastes. The country is bound to appropriate the new civilization, and the life which begins in strenuousness will be crowned with grace and charm.

If it is said that all this is idle speculation and that this picture of coming times is overwrought, it is enough to say that however far the hard actuality may fall below this height in individual cases, there can be no error in attributing mighty ethical and intellectual and æsthetic influences to the new environment of rural life. The adjustment may be slow and disappointing; it may lag in sections of the East and of the West; but the country people must change with the demand of the world, and they may yield themselves to this imperative mandate without fear. Above all we must not forget the power of the moral sentiment. As once it was dominant in the small affairs of isolated communities, exalting them to an ideal height, so ultimately it must pervade the vast industrial movement and lift humanity to its own standards. When men shall have learned to live under the new conditions without loss of leisure and personal freedom, and with the full mastery of problems that now perplex mind and heart, there may come again, at least in the country, something of the old pastoral simplicity,— something of the elementary beauty of life. And when time shall have turned promise to tradition, what is now the beauty of hope will be the long-lingering treasure of a golden age. As Bushnell found all highest worth in his age of homespun, as Pater tracked all the gods of Rome to the fields and villas, so in spite of intervals of unripeness our country towns will again satisfy the moralist and the poet.

The older virtues—frugality, self-reliance, reverence —may suffer in the new times. These qualities belong to the height of man dwelling apart and gazing into the sky doming his solitude. If the coming men, with eyes on the horizon that sweeps around their fellows, are not so tall, they are deeper-chested and better knit. The social man has taken the place of the independent man. There is now one world of the intellect even more than of industry. All thoughts are current; the printed page is the real environment of the mind. In the country there is still leisure to think,—or rather reflection may be an undertone in labor. The sensitive mind is not hustled into inactivity. It broods over deep problems. There is every reason to expect the same troop of brilliant youths to come out of the country in the future as in the past, for the rural intellect, impregnated with modern knowledge, will bring forth genius and every kind of mental superiority.

This adjustment to a new environment, gradual and, for the most part, unconscious, is not discovered until the marvel of an unexhausted and inexhaustible rural population is investigated. Then it is found that the country people are rising like an island in the sea, lifted so steadily that all the winds that blow and all the rains that fall can not waste the hills so fast as they are elevated. In the future there will be a more conscious reconstruction of institutions. The chief hindrance now is the heritage of schools and churches and an entire social structure ill adapted to a shrunken population. Time will bring new institutions, and then rural life will have every aspect of prosperity.

BOOK V

SOCIAL RECONSTRUCTION

"But he who is unable to live in society, or who has no need because he is sufficient for himself, must be either a beast or a god; he is no part of a state."

— *Jowett, " The Politics of Aristotle," Vol. I, p. 4.*

"A very strong, self-reliant people neither easily learns to act in concert, nor easily brings itself to regard any middling good—any good short of the best, as an object ardently to be coveted and striven for. It keeps its eye on the grand prizes, and these are to be won only by distancing competitors, by getting before one's comrades, by succeeding all by one's self; and so long as a people works thus individually, it does not work democratically."

—*Matthew Arnold, " Mixed Essays," p. 18.* (*Democracy.*)

"It requires generations for downtrodden people, such as those of Italy, to develop a measure of confidence which may lead them to the brave work of constructing institutions. Some of them, as for instance those of Sicily and Greece, appear to have become almost incapable of turning their considerable abilities again to such use. Their minds have lost the habit of such deeds. They have perforce become perfectly content with a narrow round of momentary actions."

—*Nathaniel Southgate Shaler, " The Individual," p. 147.*

CHAPTER XIV

THE FEDERAL PRINCIPLE

It may be well to tell the reader frankly that he will not find in this book a new Utopia. The term, social reconstruction, nevertheless, expresses more accurately than any other what here comes into view. From the beginning our study has been directed to those radical changes in our time which issue in a new social order. If in advance of this movement, when the farm household lived its independent life, and each rural community pursued its course in economic and intellectual isolation, and even political federation was at an uncertain experimental stage, some prophetic genius had divined what has actually come to pass and had published his vision, his book would have seemed as strange and alluring as Bellamy's " Looking Backward " to a later generation. The mechanical inventions by which isolation has been overcome and the rural population has taken its place in the new world order, are more wonderful than social idealist ever conceived; they could not be classed even with the wonderful forces of magic in the Arabian Nights, for they involved stranger elements than appear in those fascinating tales—forces that could not dawn upon imagination until science discovered them. Our task is not to construct a new social scheme; it is rather to complete the account of changes now in progress.

The chief distinction of our modern social structure is the application of the federal principle.[1] The world has never seen a more brilliant outburst of genius than in the Greek communities. Athens is so much better known than the other cities that one forgets how many centres of this superior life there were, until he reflects that from all the islands and shores of the Ægean and from every part of the main mass of Greece, historic names and memorials of art have survived. This region of the earth, broken and deeply indented by the sea, favored unity. The Hellenic people were no fearful sailors looking upon the waters as barriers; rather did they regard them as inviting highways of ships making every part of the Hellenic world near and accessible to every other part. Everywhere, also, these lands were occupied by a race speaking a common language, cherishing like ideals, throbbing with kindred genius. And yet these Greek communities remained isolated, disunited, rent by perpetual war, and incapable of resisting invasion, save in spasms of fraternity incited by fear. To the last the Greeks failed to discover the essential matter in the working of the federal principle.

Aristotle is an impressive witness to the distracted condition of Greece. In those portions of "The Politics" which treat of the elements of political strength he is sparing of illustrations; but when he comes to speak of revolutions, he throws upon his

[1] Cf. John Fiske, "American Political Ideals," Chap. II.

pages a picture of that shifting Greek world which reveals historical knowlege not less remarkable than his philosophical insight. Something was lacking in the political equipment of the time. It was as if atoms of metal were touched by some strange power, and, refusing to cohere, yielded but ropes of sand where should have been strong bars and chains. The missing element was the principle of representation. Only those persons who could meet in one place could share in the administration of the state. Aristotle clearly discerned the limitation of a primary assembly and accepted it without misgiving. " For the best material of democracy," he says, " is an agricultural population ; there is no difficulty in forming a democracy where the mass of the people live by agriculture or tending cattle. Being poor, they have no leisure, and therefore do not often attend the assembly." [1] As long as the effective organ of government is the primary assembly, political power can be exercised only by those who reside in the neighborhood, and whose occupation permits repeated and protracted interruptions.

Rome had remarkable success in extending her empire. Her secret lay in the generous extension of her military protection to the peoples on her borders. So urgent was the need of an international police that the surrender of independence was a cheap rate for so great a benefit. At first Rome was disposed to allow the peoples she absorbed to manage their own affairs, and she generously bestowed her citizenship upon men

[1] Jowett, " The Politics of Aristotle," Vol. I, p. 193.

from all parts of her wide domain.   Just as in Greece,
however, the representative principle was undiscovered,
and Roman statesmanship devised nothing better than
a primary assembly of the people.   The system proved
unworkable, for only the mob of the capital could
come together, and it was found necessary for the
aristocratic senate to administer the government.   It
was an easy step from such a failure in popular government to the empire.   If the provinces could have
appointed citizens to represent them and act for them,
if all parts of the empire could have continued to manage their local affairs while possessing a fair share of
responsibility and power in imperial matters, Rome
might have endured to this day.

Without the representative principle, civilization
inevitably centres in cities and cities gain political
supremacy.   In course of time the mass meeting of a
city becomes unmanageable, and revolution impends
the moment an aristocracy, forced to grasp authority,
loses control.   Rome escaped early overthrow only
because circumstances conspired to develop a huge
military power, whose benefits in maintaining peace
were greater than the evils of an aristocratic usurpa-
tion of power.   A primary assembly can never be a
match for the army, for the people assembled for
political action must always be less than the people
under arms,—the mob of a single city must be less
than the multitude of soldiers from all districts and
provinces.   An army making emperors and dethron-
ing them is more truly a democracy than a primary as-

sembly pretending to represent the people of a vast territory.

By a happy social inventiveness our ancestors in the great wilderness of Europe—rural peoples in scattered clans—bethought themselves of sending selected persons to represent them in the meeting of the tribe. This Teutonic discovery, belonging to the woods and the farms, counted for little while the political tradition of Rome prevailed. No fair field for it was found until the settlement of America opened up lands that had not felt the Roman dominion, although much of European history is concerned with the rise, or the eclipse, or the reappearance of the principle of representation.

The method of representation, which is the essential element in federal government, is a priceless part of the rural inheritance. By means of it a multitude of communities, so small as to be insignificant in themselves, are protected from encroachment and have their just share in the administration of the state and the nation. If the basis of rural prosperity is as it has been set forth in earlier parts of this discussion,—if there must be as many people in the country as in the city until the mode of sustaining life and providing for human wants changes,—then as far as the eye can dip into the future the country people, asserting themselves through the representative principle, will be influential in the republic. Without the representative principle they would sink into insignificance and be ignored in public policies; it would be necessary to revive the Greek

term, perioeci,—dwellers in the vicinity,—as if the
city only were of account.

We have seen how the country people have found
their place in the economic order of the world; in the
aggregate they stand on one side and the people of the
cities stand on the other side in the exchanges of commerce.   On that other side are a small group of cap-
italists and a huge mass of laborers.   Just now capital
and labor, with much bad temper and many outbreaks
of violence, are trying to find an agreement.   Should
they succeed, it would be possible for the amalgamated
interests to usurp control, pushing to the front manufactures and transportation, and ignoring the production of raw materials and the interests of the consumers of finished products.   There can be no fair
bargaining between individuals and collective capital,
or individuals and collective labor; much less is the
individual competent to cope with organized capital
acting in conjunction with organized labor.   The people who suffer have no way to protect themselves except through political action.   The government is the
agent of all the people, every class and condition having its fair representation; it is therefore the proper
agent to act for the people who are a majority whenever they are unable to get justice in bargaining with
a minority who have secured the perilous powers of
monopoly.   It will be found that the regulation of industrial monopolies is not an affair of the farmer nor
of the country people alone, and that there is no call
for a rural populism.   Though the country people,
being both producers of raw materials and consumers

of products, are affected more than others, multitudes in the cities have no interest in common with either organized labor or organized capital, but are deeply concerned in the distribution of products. The federal principle provides for such representation of all classes as makes the ultimate solution of these problems precisely that which the majority desires. It ought to be possible to find a solution in which the masses of the people would be sufficiently protected without checking economic development.

Professor Giddings believes that the natural line of cleavage between political parties is between the commercial, capital accumulating class on the one side, and the landowning interests of the agricultural sections and the proletarian interests of the industrial centres on the other.[1] By such an alignment the industrial movement whose strength is in the cities would recruit the party of progress, against which rural conservatism and urban poverty and incompetence would be arrayed. In Great Britain the Liberal party, in the day of its power, seemed to be such an organization of commercialism and capitalism, against which a landed aristocracy cherishing the traditional sympathy with the poor waged an unequal battle ; but this distribution of parties has passed into history, and the Conservatives are now the promoters of industrial development and of international commerce,—the old prejudice against mere shopkeeping being no longer pertinent since trade has expanded to imperial proportions. In the United States the Republican party,

[1] "The Principles of Sociology," pp. 182, 183.

which has led in industrial development, has never failed to command the support of the more prosperous agricultural sections of the North,—a fact which Professor Giddings recognizes in a footnote as an exception to his rule that the agricultural population is Democratic. The instinct of the farmer producing for the world market teaches him that his interests are conserved by those economic policies that promote urban growth and prosperity. The last thing the farmer should do is to form a party of his own, reenforced from the dispossessed of the cities, although the effort to persuade him to this folly never ceases. His true policy is to compel both parties to deserve his support by fostering those vast interests in which all the people prosper together and all share in the benefits of economic progress. Oftener than otherwise the issue between the parties will be stated in the historic terms of a loose and a strict interpretation of the constitution. When great industrial combinations demand a paternalism in the government by which they may monopolize the profits of the new social order, the farmer will stand for less interference of the government; when the weak and unorganized require protection that they may have their just share in the common possessions of civilization, he will support increased public regulation of industries. It is likely that both parties will pursue a zigzag course, offering now more and now less of paternalism, with the result that the consistent voter will find himself sometimes in one and sometimes in the other column. The country people can accomplish nothing in a party of their own, for leadership, and money, and position, and power, are in the cities ; but more important than this is the identity of interest between city and country. Freed from the domination of monopoly, the commercial and capitalistic party promotes those developments that have the largest promise of prosperity for the rural population. As long as farmers preserve one grain of sense, they will refuse a political alliance with the urban proletariat, although they will look to the cities for allies among the respectable and intelligent consumers who have no personal interest in organized capital or organized labor.

The regulation of the greater industries by government is, of course, the unsolved political problem. One may be permitted to propose such regulation without detailed explanation of its method. The problem should be approached with careful consideration of all that Herbert Spencer has suggested concerning the rights of the individual and the probable abuses of a paternal administration. Mr. Spencer himself lays the foundation for intervention in recognizing the necessity of keeping opportunity open and equal to all. " Each citizen," he says, " wants to live as fully as his surroundings permit. This being the desire of all, it results that all, exercising joint control, are interested in seeing that while each does not suffer from breach of the relations between acts and ends in his own person, he shall not break those relations in the persons of others. The incorporated mass of citizens has to maintain the condition under which each may gain the fullest life compatible with the fullest lives of fellow

citizens. . . . To maintain intact the conditions
under which life may be carried on is a business fundamentally distinct from the business of interfering with
the carrying on of the life itself, either by helping the
individual, or directing him, or restraining him."[1]

Blunders are so certainly to be feared that the chief
objection to the regulation of industries is the incompetence of government. The argument is often conducted as if the government were to make a new departure; the truth is that some of the worst evils to
be overcome are due to mistaken public policies.
Since governments have been accustomed to meddle
rashly, it may not be specially hazardous to interfere
with what wisdom—enlarged by experience—may be
at command. Nor is there here any interruption of
the evolutionary process. The same movement of evolution that develops the monopoly may develop the
public control of monopoly. A system of industrial
regulation is just as legitimate a product of evolution
as a system of laissez faire. Indeed the excesses in one
direction provoke a movement in the other, and this
is fortunate even for capital, since otherwise extortion
would overreach itself and destroy the market it
exploits.

One case is clear in the light of the principle that

[1] Herbert Spencer, "Justice," pp. 213, 214. Cf. Thorold Rogers,
"The Economic Interpretation of History," pp. 341–364. He points
out the obvious exception to the doctrine of laissez faire when all the
agents are not fairly equal in their competency to interpret their own
interests, and give effect to their interpretation. Such inequality, he
remarks, often results from former ill advised interventions of the government.

requires the intervention of the government when a strike interferes with the mails. The principle is that the mails in which all the people are concerned cannot be stopped for the settlement of a controversy in which a few of the people are concerned. Is not the case similar when a strike interferes with the supply of the necessaries of life, such as coal or beef? The interests of all the people are more important than the interests of the strikers or those who resist the strike. The government of the people, and by the people, and for the people, can do no less than arrest a strike in any industry in which there is a monopoly of the necessaries of life, providing, of course, for a judicial determination of the rights and interests in controversy.

But not to pursue the discussion of the advisability of public regulation of the industries that attain national magnitude, nothing is more certain than that the people, taking advantage of the representative principle to work their will, and profiting by the growth of the federal power, will place the business in which all have a stake under such control as they see fit to exercise,—a control far more extensive than was formerly thought of. This regulation promises radical and inspiring social changes ; one line of possible progress of vital interest to the country people may be pointed out. The first duty of the government will be to let in the light upon the great corporations. All their operations must be open to the inspection of the public which is a party in every transaction, for it is the simplest principle of trade that both parties in a bargain have a right to know the facts. As between competitor and competitor secrecy can be defended; as between a monopoly and the public, nothing can be said for it. When these great corporations are forced to act in the open, they will adopt methods that will bear inspection. The result will be the triumph of that high morality which is essential to business on the world scale. When the predatory period is over, when exploiting of ignorance has come to an end and wild experimentation and inflated development are out-grown, when industry on the world scale has settled into the solidity befitting it, the stocks of the great corporations should be as safe investments as the bonds of the government. It should be possible for indus-tries under public control to be the reservoir for the savings of the people. Provided the people can ac-cumulate savings in sufficient magnitude, they may own the great properties—the industrial plants and the railways—of the country. It is not desirable that small investors should own all the stock, and this they are not likely to do. It is better that those who possess ad-ministrative talent should control such holdings as may call out their best efforts. But here again the repre-sentative principle, under which a large number of holders of a few shares may mass their influence, has an important field.

This widely distributed ownership of the great in-dustrial properties meets the essential demand of socialism better than socialism itself. The controversy is occasioned by those great aggregations of capital which are essential to the modern system. They must be owned by a few individuals, or by many persons, or

by the state. Control by a few with the exactions
of monopoly is intolerable. Public ownership is desirable only to avert the evils of monopolistic control.
If a multitude of small investors own the active capital
of the country, there is deliverance from monopoly,
and private initiative and individual opportunity are
preserved. Ownership will be restricted to such as
exercise thrift and economy, and that certainly is preferable to taking the unthrifty and the prodigal into
one great partnership in which industry and indolence
share alike in the profits. The principle of private
ownership suffers no shock from such a system, and
land and all properties, not owned by corporations, remain in the hands of individuals. The nationalizing
of land would never have been proposed with farms in
view; were it not for the unearned increment of land
in cities and rich remnants of feudal estates, there
would be no justification of complaints concerning the
ownership of land. It costs all that a farm is worth to
make it from the wilderness. Nature is niggardly of
bounties to the farmer. It is otherwise with mines,
and routes of traffic and travel, and the market for
manufactures. These are of vast value through no
man's toil, being the gift of God and the result of
civilization. Justly they belong to all, in that state in
which they come from the hand of God ; but in their
present state after capital and labor and intelligence
without stint have been expended, they do not belong
rightfully to the people. Before the government can
take them it must pay for them, and there is no way for
the government to pay for a thing except by taxing

its citizens for the price. Taxation falls upon property or upon persons, and there seems to be no good reason why some should pay taxes in order that all in common may own these great properties. Let them be owned by those who can pay for them and will not abuse them, and all the equities of the case are met.

The point of concern to us in this discussion is, that under the system proposed the country people will become owners of large amounts of stock in the great corporations. To-day the countryman who buys stocks is a lamb, in the parlance of the initiated. The result is that one may go through whole counties and find scarcely a share of industrial or railway stocks. Instead of the interest of partners, everywhere is found the jealous and hostile feeling of those who are taxed without representation. As to the ability to make investments, the case is already clear. In great sections of the country a series of good harvests fills the banks to overflowing. The returns to agriculture are of incredible magnitude. After the support of families and the maintenance of farms and the equipment of villages, enough is left over to purchase all the stocks on the list in the course of comparatively few years. Much is now wasted because no safe and acceptable investment is at hand. If one is disposed to question this possibilty of rural savings, it is enough to point to the immense valuation of farms, largely free of mortgage, all of which in the newer parts of the country is an accumulation of a single generation. As the farms are paid for and interest charges cease, something must be done with the surplus. If the·people are to escape prodigality, it is high time that the great properties of the country were made safe depositories of savings.

Under the old system country towns profited by investments within their borders. They had shops, stores, mills, such as do not now exist. Families of wealth resided in the country more frequently than to-day, and this wealth was invested in the vicinity. What is needed now is the retention within the country town of its fair share of wealth—the ownership there of the profits of its own labor. When prosperous farmers own the stocks of the great corporations and dividends flow into the rural communities, the old condition will be recovered. This wealth is needed for the support of local institutions; it is necessary for the refinement of life, the growth of social graces, and for full participation in the prosperity of the age. Into all country towns should pour these dividends, with far greater advantage than has accrued from the distribution of the vast pension fund, since that in the main has gone to the poor and has been absorbed in the living of the people, while this stream of dividends will go to the prosperous and will add visibly to the social outfit. Nothing less than this radical redistribution of wealth without confiscation or injustice is involved in the regulation of the greater industries by government, and the plain political duty of farmers is to assert themselves through the representative principle until the federal power, vast and growing and certain to be used for ill if not for good, is made the agent and servant of all the people—the instrumentality through which they take their place in the industrial world.

In these comments upon changes in the form of society, we do little more than record the great development of the nation which is the impressive feature of the age. Not only in domestic affairs is a new federal control demanded, but in foreign relations a vigorous national policy is imperative. All the nations are awake to the need; imperialism is the order of the day. This is the inevitable consequence of a world system of industry, for the nations are gigantic industrial machines in competition. All the powers of government are drawn upon to enlarge commercial opportunity. There is a state of universal industrial war in which the forces are drilled in national camps. There is no hesitation in adding military· strength to industrial competence in the contest for national supremacy, which now means the possession of markets. The nation thus equipped and actuated is the agent of the country town in winning an opportunity to sell its products.

On the economic side, therefore, it is plain that the distinguishing element in rural life is the coming of vast benefits from without,—benefits that impose corresponding duties. The power to command these benefits depends upon the representative principle, by which each small community shares in the control of the federal activity. The economic field has been chosen for consideration here because it affords the most impressive illustration of rural enrichment from the larger life of the nation. Only that which has superlative excellence can endure the eminence of great affairs. The state therefore tends to a certain exaltation and nobility,—in contrast with the pettiness and backwardness of the small community. Being set in the state and in the nation the country town shares in the larger and higher life. It is not to be judged by what it is in itself, but by its openness to all influences of the age. In the political sphere the strength of the federal principle is the determining factor; in other spheres—education, literature, religion—a similar principle prevails. The distinction of the country town of to-day is its place in all the reciprocities that make up the rich system of the world.

CHAPTER XV

THE VITALITY OF THE TOWN

It is an interesting feature of the times that talk of imperialism excites little alarm. The tendency to enlarge the powers of government is unmistakable in many countries, and the assertion of new national strength in the international field seems to be the universal ambition. The consciousness of world relations and responsibilities awoke suddenly in the United States in connection with the Spanish war; but during the same epoch Little England was forgotten by the Empire builders, and Russia expanded beyond the line of possible peace in the Orient, and the other Great Powers sought spheres of influence in distant parts of the globe. Publicists have raised the cry of imperialism, but there is little popular sympathy with the attempt to create a reactionary movement. The people seem to look upon this national aggrandizement as an expression of their own ideals.

The reason for inattention to the warnings of anti-imperialists is that the world has passed once for all from the military to the industrial order of society. Mr. Spencer has shown how radically one system differs from the other.[1] As long as national security is at stake and the existence of a state depends upon its

---

[1] Herbert Spencer, " Justice," pp. 184-190, and elsewhere.

ability to cope with its neighbors in war, it is necessary to sacrifice individual rights and to ignore local interests in order that the whole power of the united citizens may be available. A military government of high centralization inevitably results. When, on the other hand, the world has advanced beyond the chronic state of war and has given itself to the industries that enrich life, the great desideratum is that the individual should be free to work out the best that he can conceive. An industrial society demands liberty as decisively as a military society forbids it. The world having advanced to the industrial stage, militarism is no longer feared.

There is a further reason for the refusal of the people to be alarmed—the federal power is a thing of their own creation. Authority mounts upward from the people; it does not descend from thrones. Whatever may be the growth of centralization, it leaves local self-government unimpaired. These two opposites— federal power and local administration, the national government and the town-meeting—cohere in one system. If we were hastening on toward real imperialism, the sign would be a diminishing participation of the people in local government. It is known that nothing of the sort appears, and therefore the expansion of national interests is regarded with complacency. "Americans," writes their great interpreter and critic, "constantly reply to the criticism which Europeans pass on the faults of their State legislatures and the shortcomings of Congress by pointing to the healthy efficiency of their rural administration, which enables them to bear with composure the defects of the higher organs of government." [1]

The settlement of New England—to a less extent this appears elsewhere—was by communities. There is now a striking difference between America and Europe in rural life. In Europe the country people are more generally gathered in villages; in America more of them are scattered over the whole face of the country, dwelling on their farms. Early New England resembled Europe. For obvious reasons the settlers did not disperse to farmsteads: they needed protection; they valued the fellowship of religion; they planned for the education of their children. They found it advisable, therefore, to live in clusters of houses around the common fort, the common church, the common school. If we ask why it was so easy for them to adopt this village life, the answer is that this social organism was an inheritance. Centuries of semi-communistic agriculture had formed their ideals and instincts. In the Middle Ages the people grouped their houses, distributed their arable land in narrow strips, held pastures and woodlands in common, and when crops were removed, drove their united herds and flocks to the fenceless fields. The village was an agricultural community, united in an intricate social order. Whether the land originally belonged to the community or to the lord of the manor; whether there was a primitive socialism or a primitive feudalism, may never be known. It matters little for our purpose whether the strips of land were distributed in a village

[1] James Bryce, "The American Commonwealth," Vol. I, p. 591.

meeting or rented of the local lord ; in either case there was a real community bound together by the closest ties.[1] The first New England settlements retained many vestiges of this old rural socialism.

The early New England town-meetings were possible because the settlers were of the stock which had once enjoyed a highly socialistic training. In a new country they quickly appropriated the greater part of the civic functions, exercising powers that have not been claimed in recent times. The assignment of lands, the regulation of agriculture, defense against the Indians, the maintenance of religion, fell to the towns. Whatever authority belonged to the lord of the manor had no duplicate in the wilderness ; courts of wider jurisdiction were not available at the first; colonial—not to say national—government developed slowly. The town-meeting came into existence with unique responsibilities and powers. It was the most perfect local democracy that the world has ever seen ; it was also the source of the delegated authority of the colonial assembly. It did not receive its charter from the central authority, but parted with its power to constitute a common government of towns in the same region.

[1] For a thorough account of the agricultural community of the later middle ages Frederic Seebohm's " The English Village Community " may be consulted. Careful investigations cast doubt upon an original democracy at the base of English institutions—that source of local self-government of which historians have made much. Seebohm finds the lord of the manor in control of vassals from the earliest times and describes the life of our ancestors as a communistic serfdom. In any case the close social organization was dominant for centuries.

Necessarily this robust offspring of the wilderness lost vigor as time passed. Judicial functions soon passed to more comprehensive courts. Military independence was impracticable after the first exigencies. Land titles became the care of the General Court under provisions of law, with local registry—in town or county—telling the tale of origins. Long ago religion ceased to be supported and controlled by the towns, being surrendered to voluntary societies. There has been a loss of functions on the one hand to the county, the state, and the nation, and on the other hand to voluntary societies and individuals.

In yet another way the town has suffered. In course of time the whole territory was occupied, as families pushed out upon the farms. This shattered the social solidity; it broke the closeness of acquaintance, altered the habit of coöperation, and tended to develop an unsocial individuality. Then came the splitting of the town into school districts, which became centres for a new social crystallization with much sectional isolation and antagonism. Worse than all else was the rupture of the church, crossing the sectional with sectarian lines and making a maze in which society was lost.

When these changes had run their course, the town was very different from what it had been in the days when it was the one vital political institution in the beginnings of a nation. As new regions were settled, they grew up in the later municipal feebleness rather than in the old social strength. In most cases there was no original social body—no village with school, and church, and neighborly life. The individual was first, the community afterward. From the start the school district had the right of way, and any sect that could sustain itself pressed in, to the confounding of the ecclesiastical order. There was too much individualism, too much sectionalism, too much sectarianism, too much of clique and faction; and if a town meeting was held, the town affairs were of little importance and awakened a slight interest once a year.

The changes in population, it need not be said, have weakened the towns throughout the depleted area. Not only are they relatively less powerful in consequence of the growth of cities, but there is a sensible loss of social force within their borders. A smaller number of people cannot keep the old machinery running at full speed. Social institutions as well as the social feeling require a certain density of population. If the people are thinned beyond that point, social disintegration threatens : schools become too small for proper organization and for enthusiasm ; churches struggle hopelessly or surrender to insuperable difficulties ; even the town-meeting succumbs to the universal discouragement as the voters no longer crowd the hall and the tax-list shortens.

Many towns are injured, also, by the proximity of stronger industrial and social centres. Their citizens go abroad for trade, for acquaintance, for social fraternization, and even for school and church. They look to the adjacent thriving village or city as their true centre with consequent alienation from their own

political and social circle. The trolley widens the
sphere of this influence; the rural delivery of mails
diminishes contact with the village; the telephone,
though it unites the people, keeps them apart also.
The whole story is not told in these terms, but they
merit consideration for so much of truth as is in them.

In view of all the facts—the evident social decay of
some towns and the loss of relative importance by all
—the question becomes urgent, Is any social reconstruction possible by which these cells of democracy
may be recharged? Two courses are open—the
social unit may be enlarged, or its vitality may be
increased.

The remark was made by President Dwight that the
towns of New England were too small.[1] He regarded
the endless reduplication of petty offices, the division
of affairs into minute sections lacking dignity and
impressiveness, as wasteful and ineffective. If this
was a just impression a century ago, it can hardly be
avoided to-day. Yet it is probably a merely academic
question whether the size of towns might be increased.
The natural limit is that of convenience in attending
the town meeting. Two towns with scant population
within easy reach of a suitable point on their common
border might unite with profit; but boundaries have
been fixed unalterably, in many cases, by the configuration of the land—in other instances quite as
irrevocably by the conservatism of the people. The
most favorable opportunity for consolidation is that in

[1] Timothy Dwight, LL. D., "Travels in New England and New
York," New Haven, 1821, Vol. I, p. 176.

which new political bounds would conform to an accomplished social readjustment. Here and there the trolley prepares the way for changes of this kind, and the growth of new industrial centres suggests that the old custom of perambulating the bounds of the town at intervals might yield practical benefit with sagacious officials making the circuit.

Little relief being promised from the enlargement of towns, an alternative is found in the greater use of the county as the local administrative unit. From the beginning there have been two methods of local self-government in the United States—the town system and the county system. Just as naturally as the town-meeting sprang into life in New England, the county developed in Virginia. The great plantations connected by the rivers at once made the local community impossible and lent themselves to the county organization. The convenient meeting places were the centres of districts large enough for small counties. The emigrants from Virginia carried the county with them, just as the emigrants from New England established the town and the town-meeting. A northern belt of states has the town system, and a southern belt of states has the county system—the intermediate region having a mingling of the two modes of organization.

It might be supposed that in the weakening of the town the county would come to new favor; this seems not to be the case. The county serves while population is thin; there is little reversion to it when population is depleted. The county is a temporary expedient, rather than a final institution, except for judicial purposes. The reason why the county cannot hold its place in local administration is, that it is too large for a primary assembly and too small for a representative legislature. The care of the insane, for example, in some states has been given to counties. This is inadvisable because there is no means of calling the commissioners to account. If the insane are wards of the state, the legislature may order an investigation and grievances may be redressed. The town would have the same kind of control, but the unit is too small to provide proper care and treatment. Without a legislative body to direct executive officers, government becomes an oligarchy; because there can be no such assembly in the county, it is not suited to serve as the political unit of democracy. The ultimate unit of popular government must be the group of citizens that can conveniently assemble. The city presents a more difficult problem than that of distance, for when the assembly numbers more than a thousand, deliberate parliamentary action becomes impracticable. It is necessary to divide the city into wards and to provide for a representative assembly. A true democracy would require a similar provision if the county were made the unit of administration. The popular assembly has been regarded as the school of the people in self-government, and it would be an almost fatal blow to democracy to close it. Because the town has been given boundaries in accordance with the demands of an assembly of the people, the wisdom of the town organization is evident, and there is a slow substitution of the town system for the county system in the West and even in the South.[1]

The balance of our political system is preserved by the strengthening of the town and the state, which together stand for local self-government against nationalism. The state tends to become a mere shell of officialdom. If all functions of the county—except the judicial—which are too great for the towns, are transferred to the state, there is a substantial gain, for somewhere there must be a massing of the forces of local self-government to make head against what, if unchecked, would be national imperialism. The British system lacks the state, which is the distinctive excellence of our political organization. To scatter the functions of the state among counties, that never can become political forces of adequate magnitude, is as unwise as to concentrate in counties the functions of towns. Our true system is that of town, state, and nation, each equipped with executive and legislative powers ; and the prospect is that this typical form will become universal,—the county serving as a temporary mode of organization, somewhat as the territorial government is a passing provision for newly settled regions.

This survey yields the result that the town, with boundaries unchanged for the most part, is a vital and permanent factor of our political system. Although many forces tend to weaken the towns, some secret power working in history, which can be nothing else than the spirit of democracy, counteracts the disinte-

[1] For a careful study of the town and county systems see, " John Hopkins University Studies," Vol. I.

gration. This vigor of the town, this conquering march across the continent, should have its true valuation in any review of rural institutions.

Within the town one most notable change has taken place. The strain upon institutions resulting from depletions was first apparent in the district schools. Many schools that once had scores of pupils became too small for profitable continuance. The financial burden upon the poorer districts suggested a more economical and more equitable method; it is probable, indeed, that common sense in adjusting taxes had quite as much to do with the downfall of the district system as any pedagogical considerations. The assumption of the support of all the schools within its limits by the town and the provision for their administration by a single school board, is an educational revolution of the first magnitude. The single district school was too slight a thing to command serious attention, and as long as the system lasted, it was impossible to make any advance in the direction in which the normal schools were leading. The combined educational interests of an entire town are a different matter; the field is large enough, and responsibility is definite enough, to assure the attention and the careful oversight that promise improvement. Some of the smaller schools have been given up; here and there a more radical course has been followed,—the schools of a town being consolidated and graded. It is found entirely practicable to assemble the children in a central school, for transportation proves cheaper than the multiplication of schools of the same grade. Experiments of this kind are now so numerous and so well known and their result is so convincing that the method of improving the rural schools is plain to all who have eyes to see. The town system of administration is everywhere practicable, and consolidation and gradation have wide opportunity. The educational gains of these changes are beyond calculation ; and better methods, and the enthusiasm of numbers, and the new sense of dignity promise for the country school a development that will make it for the coming time as effective as the much lauded district school in the old days.

The social consequences of this new method in education are here to be pointed out. The town itself gains dignity and importance as a political institution. Taking up the educational function, the town almost doubles its public business, and this by the addition of purely intellectual and moral elements. A town-meeting gains more elevation from a discussion of schools than from a discussion of roads. As soon as a public sentiment in favor of improved schools is developed and pride in the schools is justified, the community has a new social consciousness. Here is a co-operation of the finest kind, giving the people a common thought, a common object of devotion, and a common spirit of sacrifice. The consolidated school has powerful influence for good : the children from different sections are educated together ; their acquaintance is wide as the town ; life for them is in a larger world ; they escape the provincialism of the remote school district. Children growing up with the town con-

sciousness promise much for the uplift and enrichment
of the community.

The library easily follows the introduction of an
efficient school system. Privately established and endowed a library should be, for its provision and maintenance are too costly for taxation alone ; but however
founded and sustained a library for all the people
should be in their control. This again adds to the
functions of the town government a most honorable
and ennobling element.

The state can do much in inspiring and assisting the
town in providing schools and libraries. The school
laws, the normal school, and the distribution of
the state school tax do much to overcome inertia
and ignorance in backward towns; yet always the
aim is to arouse and aid the local forces. The state
takes the initiative when necessary, and this tendency is increasingly manifest.[1] It seems in no way to

[1] Matthew Arnold saw in the state the desirable complement of
democracy. Recognizing the passing of aristocracy—the old seat and
source of high reason and right feeling—and perceiving the poverty
of democracy in ideals of loftiest worth, he looked to the state to
supply what shall ennoble the modern world. "The State can bestow
certain broad collective benefits, which are indeed not much if compared with the advantages already possessed by individual grandeur,
but which are rich and valuable if compared with the make-shifts of
mediocrity and poverty" (Mixed Essays, p. 32. Democracy). He
illustrates his view by an earnest advocacy of state control of education. He supposes that a single community, under the domination of
democracy, will lack interest and intelligence for the high task of
educating itself, and that an adequate zeal and proper methods must
be communicated from outside. For this the collective wisdom of all
the people is demanded.

arrest the town development. In striking contrast with this experience in the educational field is the growing favor of local option in states which have tried a general prohibitory liquor law. The aim in state prohibition has been the same as in educational leadership—to bring to bear upon the community living on the lower level the ideal of the higher levels on which the life of a state moves. We but record the result of experiment when we say that—for good or ill—states are more and more leaving the determination of policy in this matter to the towns. This accords with that general reinvigoration of the town which we are tracing. Local option, however, should not apply to the enforcement of law, for the alternative of enforcement is nullification. The authority of the state seems to be necessary in securing obedience to the will of the people expressed in the vote of the town, and police officers and prosecuting attorneys and judges do their duty best when independent of local support and directly responsible to some department of the state government. In fact town and state and nation tend to increase their functions as society develops and individualism is outgrown; we claim for the town only that it vigorously maintains its place in the political system.

This is not the place to consider the growing unity of the church, nor the many forces that help to transform a mass of persons into a social group. Influences never definitely recognized in town-meeting have a very important part in the vitality of the town, but they cannot be treated in this chapter, which deals with the town as a political institution.

It is inspiring to find the town demonstrating its vitality and its political competence. If half the people are to live in the country, their retention of the spirit and the primary institutions of democracy is of inestimable value to the republic. When it is added that a multitude of the influential citizens of the great centres have their birth and training in country towns, it is evident that true democracy in the town-meeting goes far to preserve true democracy in the nation. This diffused and pungent spirit, building everywhere the institutions of local self-government, is the corrective of any excesses of nationalism and the assurance that imperialism is not an immediate danger. We may indulge the hope that the town-meeting will use the federal principle and control the federal power as long as the republic endures.

CHAPTER XVI

THE PRESERVATION OF THE CHURCH

THE Christian church began in cities. Jerusalem,
Antioch, Ephesus, Corinth, Rome, marked its line of
conquest. The Jews, who opened the way for the
gospel, were inhabitants of cities. While the converts
were but a few in thousands of the people, the rural
districts could not have churches. When Christianity
won imperial support and the problems of life in a
pagan society became acute, earnest Christians in large
numbers fled to lonely places, and monastic communities grew up around those whose piety was most
celebrated. In the cities the old social life secularized
the church; in the country it kept aloof from the
groups where faith ruled. Until the Reformation the
church was imperial and monastic, rather than democratic and rural. The Reformation followed the track
of the Renaissance and commerce; it was a town
movement and only slowly and imperfectly reached
the country people. Notable is the sense of novelty
when Wesley and his followers preached to the masses
of England,—novelty because the people had never
been evangelized quite as much as because of the fresh
statement of the gospel. Even a century ago Robert
Hall preached a sermon on " The Present Crisis " in
which he drew a dark picture of the times, declaring

that throughout the kingdom the number of people regularly assembling for public worship was far inferior to those who neglected it. By this time evangelistic zeal had told upon the rural population, bad as was its religious condition; in the great cities not one-fourth of the people attended public worship, and in the metropolis the proportion was much less than this beggarly fraction. All the exact information that has come down to us suggests a condition of the churches in strange contrast with that golden age that shines so alluringly in tradition. There was never a time when all the country people went to church and were faithful and devout Christians.

In New England there was an extraordinary religious homogeneity in some of the towns for a time. The religious motive, where it determined the migration, drew a body of people of like faith and ideals; and these religious men and women, being separated from the rest of the world, constituted communities in which virtually all shared in public worship and wrought together to establish a reign of God on earth. It happens naturally enough that the history of the founding of New England cannot be told without putting these communities into the great and memorable chapters. In other parts of the land, also, the religious foundations have been conspicuous and influential. The result is that our poor present must be shamefaced in the comparison with the past, like the humble descendant of a patrician ancestor whose choice strain is swamped by scores of unions with inferior stock.

We are entitled to whatever comfort there is in a full account of the process by which we came to be what we are. The New World was settled from the Old World, and necessarily all sorts of people came,—if not in one ship, in another. A half pagan country could not send forth a perfectly Christian exodus. A writer of much discrimination and of unusual information, speaking of all the colonies, points out the " godless fringe to the pious garment . . . a host of the shiftless, ne'er-do-well, or positively vicious kind, who naturally found in a new country some relief from the restraints and some respite from the fruitless toil of the fatherland." [1] There was more than a fringe of godlessness. Not to repeat what has been set forth in treating " The Heritage of Unfitness," it may be enough to say that there is no mystery of iniquity in the present neglect of the church by approximately half of the country people; this is the legitimate historical sequence. We are needlessly disheartened when we compare the present with a time when all the people were patterns of the Christian virtues. Nothing is more remarkable than the extent to which later generations forget.[2]

---

[1] Frank B. Sanborn, " New Hampshire," p. 29.

[2] The tradition of a more prosperous life in the churches is strong in the region most familiar to the writer. Yet a careful historian, writing only thirty years after the date named, to whom the facts must have been known, says : " In most of the towns in the eastern part of Rockingham and Strafford Counties, the institutions of religion failed to be early established, or have been feebly sustained. Out of twenty-seven or twenty-eight towns in this section of the state, there were

Needless alarm has been excited by telling the tale of religious changes as if the present as men now behold it were in contrast with a past as an idealizing imagination reconstructs it. We shall not pursue the investigation,—being content to record the opinion that

found at the end of two centuries not more than five towns affording an adequate support for the preached gospel; while in the adjoining county of Strafford, of the thirty-five or thirty-six towns then included within its limits, but three towns were found in the year 1826, furnishing an adequate support to the Christian ministry."—Robert F. Lawrence, " The New Hampshire Churches," p. 12.

An appeal presented to the New Hampshire Home Missionary Society in 1823 names eighteen towns in Strafford County in which the Congregational societies "are entirely broken to pieces," and adds that in other towns they maintain a doubtful and precarious existence. See the able report of Secretary Alfred T. Hillman at the centenary of the society (Minutes of the General Association of the Congregational Churches of New Hampshire, 1901).

" Only the shell of orthodoxy was left in 1800," Henry Adams, " History of the United States," Vol. I, p. 90,—a gross exaggeration, but wholesome to think of when the optimistic tradition becomes oppressive.

The decline of the churches, so far as it is real, belongs to the recent cycle of change and does not date from an early idyllic period. Twenty-three towns of Rockingham County share in the depletion, common to the older agricultural towns, losing in fifty years about one-third of their Protestant population. In such conditions the weakening of the churches need not excite surprise; surprise is due rather to the fact that the Congregational churches of these towns lost not more than half as great a percentage of their members as the towns lost of their people during this trying half century.

In this chapter, as elsewhere, the author uses facts with which he is most familiar in the hope that a disproportionate reference to his own state and denomination will not be construed as provincial and sectarian. This, of course, is permissible only where illustration and not conclusive argument is sought.

many pessimistic conclusions concerning the religious condition of country towns start from the false premise that all country towns were once profoundly religious.

In treating of social reconstruction the problem of the preservation of the church is of more concern than the true tracing of its history,—the comparison with the past being of service only as it affords warning or encouragement. On the supposition that people of many characters formed the original communities and that the beginnings of the church were often feeble, the gain from dispelling the charge of degeneracy is offset by the burden of an unfortunate inheritance. Just because idyllic conditions did not prevail in early times, it is unsafe to relax diligence in the present. And this would be true if in all other respects there were prosperity. Grave is the danger when rural communities, far too little influenced by religion in the beginning, suffer such changes as have been described in the earlier sections of this discussion.

Growing towns have their peculiar phase of this problem. If the strangers are religious, their assimilation in existing churches is slow and difficult; often it is disappointing, for the Christian does not always bear transplanting well. An aggressive newcomer sometimes runs an exciting career until the adherents of old customs teach him his place, or he succeeds in shaking them out of their habits. The mingling of diverse elements, though beneficial on the whole, is doubtless the explanation of much of the ecclesiastical friction of the time. But the strangers may not be re-

ligious, and this may be the case with the native as
well as the foreign migrant.   Before our towns began
to grow, the surrounding population was largely irreligious, so that accessions from the vicinity were by
no means certain to strengthen the churches.   The
times, also, tend to develop a roaming class as devoid
of religion as the rolling stone of moss.   And more
significant still, the growing town may have an influx
of foreigners of no religion, or of a faith demanding
religious institutions of its own.   Protestant churches,
certainly, do not find their opportunity enlarged when
a Roman Catholic invasion gives the town a favorable
showing in the census.   The real strain upon religious
institutions may be as great in a changing as in a
diminishing population.   In cities an enormous growth
brings religious problems to an acute stage, for the
old Protestant churches find themselves without a constituency at the seats of their former power and are
compelled to follow their retreating supporters into
the suburbs.   However heartily the service of the
Roman Catholic church in caring for the horde of immigrants may be appreciated, one cannot fail to see
that the maintenance and development of churches and
their social power are far different from what would
be expected in a homogeneous population.

The purpose of this chapter, however, is not to discuss the problem of churches in growing communities,
urban or rural; nor is there special need of such discussion, for it may be presumed that where general
prosperity is most evident, there will be no failure to
share in that religious growth which all comprehensive

statistics demonstrate.[1] The strain may be great and drastic readjustments may be necessary, but the churches as a whole grow more rapidly than the population, and the Protestant churches are in the van of this religious progress. When we turn from the growing to the depleted communities, conditions of another sort appear, and the preservation of the churches in this sharp trial is an urgent and vital problem.

The churches in those towns which have lost from ten to forty per cent. of their people within fifty years have suffered a severe strain. In the more populous towns and the more religious communities strong churches have been weakened; what then must be the experience where the people never were numerous, and the institutions of religion never were vigorous?

---

[1] Comparing the whole population (United States) with the total evangelical communicants, we have these striking results:

1800	one communicant in	14.50	inhabitants.
1850	"	"	" 6.57 "
1870	"	"	" 5.78 "
1880	"	"	" 5.00 "
1890	"	"	" 4.53 "
1900	"	"	" 4.28 "

—Rev. Daniel Dorchester, D. D., *The Congregationalist*, December 29, 1900, p. 977.

No possible revision or interpretation of this table, in which Dr. Dorchester sums up and supplements the investigations recorded in his "Problem of Religious Progress" (p. 594) and "Christianity in the United States" (p. 755) can obliterate the evidence of an amazing religious advance. Rarely do statistics march in such a triumphal procession as in the article from which the table is taken. The work first named cites many contemporary authorities concerning the spiritual declension during the eighteenth century. See pp. 381–406.

That the supporters of churches leave the rural communities in exceptional numbers is probable, for they are quick to hear the call of larger opportunity and greater service in the degree in which they have received the Christian spirit. Certainly the greater number of those who pass into the ampler world by the highway of education have felt the stimulus of the church in their plastic childhood. When, therefore, depletion has run its course a weaker church is in a more irreligious community, unless other forces change the result. Obviously there must be many sad examples of spiritual and moral decay,—bewailed justly enough, but rightly interpreted as consequences of industrial changes. Innumerable witnesses voice lamentation and criticism, to whom we must listen, although what they deplore is part of the progress of the age.

The preservation of the churches in depleted towns calls for heroic measures. Of these the most certain to occur to every mind is the consolidation of enfeebled organizations. There is a limited sphere within which the consolidation of farms is demanded; there is a wide-spread movement for the consolidation of schools; why should the children of light alone fail to read the meaning of the times? The melancholy multiplication of churches is known to all; viewed from the social side, the division of the people, the splitting up of resources, the poverty and feebleness of congregations, the meagre equipment, the unholy competitions and jealousies, the utter failure to inspire and lead the community, constitute an arraignment of the common sense and Christianity of those responsible for this condition against which defense is impossible. Fortunately the case has been appealed to a higher court, and churches that cannot vindicate their right to existence are compelled to surrender to the new order of civilization. The people being too few, the number of churches must be reduced.

Thus far a strange and reprehensible stubbornness has given this promising movement a grim look. Churches have chosen to die in independence rather than yield in season to a prudent consolidation. This clears the field, but the process is painful and perilous, for religion may perish while the struggling churches are waiting for their competitors to expire. To persist in a forlorn hope when union would help the higher life of the community, to prolong the struggle for existence until the death of the weaker church determines to which contestant the field belongs, is a spectacle that might be expected on the low levels of evolution, but ought never to be witnessed in the high places where love and fellowship are the ruling forces of civilization. And when a church is extinct, its house of worship falling into ruin, remains to lend its sombre suggestions to the itinerant pessimist. So many of these abandoned edifices have provoked lamentation that one who appreciates their true meaning may take heart. The elimination of superfluous churches is well under way. The most divisive and the least serviceable succumb. So great is this ecclesiastical mortality that a writer who has a sharp eye for it has boldly given his article the title, " The Passing of the Country

Church." [1]   The crossroads come-outers are the first to
go.   Indeed by the country church this observer
seems to mean the church by the highway or in some
petty hamlet.

The dissolution of churches may go far before real
harm is done.   At the centenary of the New Hampshire Home Missionary Society in 1901, the fact was
brought to light that in twenty-eight towns Congregational churches had ceased to exist without
apparent injury, inasmuch as forty Protestant churches
and one Roman Catholic church still survived. [2]   It is
a fair inference that these churches died because they
served no useful purpose.   There is little occasion to
fear that the older parts of the country will ever have
too few churches.   In Vermont the last decade developed a surprising mortality of churches ; but more
remarkable is the founding of new organizations,—
eleven Protestant denominations making good their
own losses, filling the gap created by the loss of
twenty-four churches in six other denominations, and
finally swelling the total number by thirty-five. [3]   It
would seem evident that churches die only where they
are not needed, and that they spring into being where
they are required by changes in population.   It is
difficult, also, to resist the impression that just as they
linger too long where mortality is desirable, so they
multiply too easily where sectarian propagandism discovers a chance to repeat its old folly.   Here and there

[1] James E. Boyle, *The Outlook*, May 28, 1904, p. 234.
[2] Op. Cit., p. 59.
[3] Rev. John M. Comstock, *The Congregationalist*, April 20, 1901.

towns are relieved of superfluous organizations, although we have to record a delay of the better order that tries our patience. How much wiser than the sinking of the feeblest to extinction would be the masterly meeting of the situation by a consolidation of organizations while there is a fair measure of strength !

That a vast change in the institutional outfit of depleted towns is in progress through the elimination of superfluous churches, and that the union of living churches has great possibilities, will not be questioned; yet if we had nothing to suggest but waiting for inevitable death, or working for union with inevitable defeat, with justice our programme would be pronounced unpractical. A great number of churches will live, and the inquiry presses, By what means can they increase their hold on life ? Many churches that will triumph ultimately are now in grave danger; how can they make their preservation sure ? The reliance must be upon means and measures as well as upon the great assurances of faith.

We may begin with an inventory of resources. There is, first of all, a more primitive piety in the country than in the city. And this is in three forms —the mystical experience, the ethical application in the personal life, and the revival interest. Comparative leisure and solitude favor that musing in which mysticism lives; the absence of great social problems permits the concentration of the moral effort upon individual relations; and partly through the influence of tradition, less disturbed in the country, and partly in

consequence of the mystical bent, it is never difficult
to gather a little circle of believers to pray and yearn
for the conversion of souls.

Allied to this apostolic type of piety is a special
interest in theology. In the country there is less
popular impatience with doctrine and more concern
for systems of thought; there is less demand that the
preacher should set his note-book to catch the drift-
wood on the literary stream, and more desire that he
should enter the forest and with his own ax cut down
the living tree. In many lives there is a continuous
effort to reach a solution of the problems of duty and
of thought—an undertow of meditation setting toward
the deep sea. Rural congregations believe in a plan
of redemption.

Further, there is in the country a better use of social
tradition, in a fashion thoroughly scientific though
developed unconsciously. The children attend the
services of the church; the adults are present in the
Sunday-school. There is less shirking of religious
training by parents, and less scorning of parents by
Sunday school autocrats. Family prayers are the rule
in Christian households,—at least this is still the case
where the older ways are undisturbed. The child
grows up in a religious atmosphere, charged with the
influence of mature persons who command respect,
and with the vital forces of the parental example. Acquaintance is so general and so intimate that personality has extraordinary impressiveness and unhindered
opportunity. There is less distraction in the country
and more chance for an accumulating social and per-

sonal influence. The result of all these conditions and forces is a vital tradition of religion, through which the church molds generation after generation and maintains its place of power in the community.

Such assets as these should place churches even in depleted communities far above spiritual bankruptcy, —with the exception, of course, of those superfluous organizations which have the peculiar opportunity to bless the world by their death. The possibilities of heredity and nurture exceed the common expectation,—an example may show how great they are. More than fourscore years ago a man and his wife joined a Congregational church in Vermont. Six of their seven children became members of that church —the oldest son dying while in college with the ministry in view. Of thirty-one grandchildren twenty became members of this church, and seven others members of Congregational churches elsewhere. At one time eight of the grandchildren were members of the choir, and thirty were members of the Sunday-school. It must be added that when this item was published one solitary representative of this family was left in the old church. Had the great-grandchildren taken their places in this succession, the way to build a church would be perfectly clear, for two faithful persons for a beginning, with heredity and nurture, would make a church in course of time. Not often is this instance paralleled either in its fruitfulness or in the final dispersion. The ordinary country church has a nucleus of some half dozen families in which the tradition of piety triumphantly illustrates the promises of

God, enough of whose children remain to preserve the succession. From this choice stock come the leaders of the church, of whom there may be three or four men and twice as many women. In many cases there is one man who for thirty or forty years holds the church together, puts the stamp of his spirit upon it, and makes it the larger embodiment of his own life. Slender, indeed, is this vital thread, and it is not strange that here and there it breaks with disaster to the church. In the city these leaders may be imported; in the country they must be bred. Fortunately it is possible for the whole force of the Christian family and the Christian church to be received into the heart of the child with that growth into spiritual power which furnishes to the world a Christian leadership. While this process lasts, the country church will live; when it comes to an end, there will be times of trouble through which prophecy discerns no way. The effort must be directed towards the perpetuation of those influences under which a man and a woman, entering the church to-day, may be the founders of one of these fruitful Christian households.

The theological opportunity in the country is underestimated. It is a familiar charge that an excessive conservatism prevents the growth of the country church, and it is a frequent ambition of young men just out of their theological incubation to win whole communities to the church by heralding their new interpretations of truth. Invariably these enthusiasts suffer disillusion, and the reason for this is not the conservatism of the churches to which they minister. It is rather the indifference of those who are supposed to be in the quest of a spiritual philosophy. The best illustration is found in the young preacher's experience with Biblical criticism. He imagines that a general welcome awaits his deft removal of the difficulties in the Old Testament and his new version of the story of the gospels. To his amazement he finds that the people to whom he throws open the doors pay no heed. The explanation of their unconcern is simple enough, for when the Bible is no longer read, its difficulties are not felt. Yet a few thoughtful Bible readers and Bible-believers feel deeply the perplexities that criticism resolves, and there is no place in the world where the new interpretation of the Bible, judiciously presented, will be so warmly welcomed as in the Bible class of a country Sunday school. It should be remembered, of course, that it takes twenty years, at least, to make the transition from the old to the new view ; a hundred presuppositions must change, a hundred new points of view must be gained, before the mind rests in the comfort and assurance that criticism offers. To expect a sudden acceptance of critical dogmas is folly ; there must be patient waiting for the work of time, and our contention is that the interest in theological thinking is so keen in the rural church that the preparation for new light, always in progress, affords an unrivalled opportunity for the thoughtful and wise Christian teacher. The constructive interest sets limits to the proposals that will be entertained, but there is no reason to doubt that the average rural congregation would take kindly to the positive elements in such a programme as that suggested by President William D. Hyde.[1] Even when the attack on the old theology is resented, there are a dozen who are indignant at misrepresentation, as that they believe in " an absentee and ancient God," to one who is aroused by the challenge of his own faith. It may be confidently affirmed that whatever advantage belongs to the reconstruction of theology need not be forfeited in the country church. That many country ministers and many country churches construe Christianity in antiquated terms is not denied; our claim is that the field is open for modern ministers, and that because it is open and will be entered, the country church shares in whatever hopes wait upon the intellectual tendencies of the times. If there is less alertness, there is more meditation than in the city; and if demolition is slower, construction is easier.

Great as is the power of family and social tradition, and hopeful as is the theological outlook, the emphasis should fall upon the missionary spirit in speaking of the preservation of the church in the depleted town. This is the proper expression of that more primitive piety which we have recognized as the rural type; but it is also the fruit of that more friendly theology to which all men are children of God, and it is the saving salt that prevents hereditary piety from developing a patrician spirit. It is not too much to say that the missionary spirit guarantees the perpetuation of the church, and that without much regard to the loss of

[1] "The Social Mission of the Country Church," Minutes of the National Council of the Congregational Churches, 1901, pp. 223–232.

population. It must be remembered that around every church is a large missionary field—this being an incidental benefit of the mixture of population from the beginning. The irreligious population invites Christian interest and prayer and labor. As long ago as 1886, the author reached the conclusion that a church might hope to grow in a declining town, and all that has come under observation since has failed to overthrow the conviction that more depends upon the vitality and the activity of the church than upon the fortune of the town in keeping or losing its people. At that time the membership of the Congregational churches of Vermont as reported in the Year-book of 1855 was compared with what was then the latest report, and it was found that of 108 churches in towns that lost in population from 1850 to 1880, forty-nine showed an increased membership. This accords with the result reached by another student of these churches who found that of 123 Congregational churches in towns which declined between 1880 and 1890, fifty-five gained in membership during that decade. Facts like these, without carrying the investigation into other states and other denominations, suffice to break the force of that fatalistic despair that haunts the mind when thinking of churches in depleted towns. Naturally a church in a declining town should lose in membership; that such is the experience even in a majority of cases calls for no comment. The surprising thing is that in these churches in Vermont the law of gain and loss apparently bears no relation to the growth and depletion of the towns in which they are located ; evidently it must take account of spiritual forces—the social tradition, the theological interest, the missionary enthusiasm.

One phase of local missionary activity deserves special mention. Nearly every country church is surrounded by remote districts within its field. Experience shows that comparatively few persons will attend church if they must travel more than three miles. It is possible for the church to be interested in the people when they are not interested, or seem not to be interested in the church. In this case it is feasible for the church to seek the people with that combination of personal and public work that almost never fails. A neighborhood meeting in a schoolhouse or a convenient residence will secure a quite general attendance. The definiteness of the invitation, the thorough canvass of households, the local pride, the perfect acquaintance of the people with one another, indifference to dress, the entire absence of ecclesiasticism and sectarianism, the perfect simplicity of the conditions repeating the environment of the primitive church, contribute to an often surprising result, profitable to the people of the vicinity and refreshing to the pastor and his helpers. The reaction of such work upon the spiritual life is most valuable, for prayer is stimulated; faith is quickened; the spirit of friendliness is cultivated; the venture and the activity take the church out of ruts and give the flush of red blood in motion. The principle involved is more important than appears at first. Many a schoolboy finds the story of Cæsar's conquest of Gaul dull reading because he does not see that the great statesman's far-sighted enterprise saved decadent Rome by gaining a new constituency. To-day every great nation is awake to the importance of securing new territory and establishing intercourse with new peoples. The country church has a providential opportunity to apply the principle that has saved nations and is remaking the world. The field of the church is enlarged; but this is not all, for there is a steady drift of individuals and families towards the central village. It means much when young men and women take service in the nearer homes, when boys and girls attend the village school, when a family yields to the constant gravitation—that they are known to the pastor and his helpers and feel a friendliness towards the church; that they come from a girdle of Christian neighborhoods rather than from a fringe of pagan settlements. Thus within a little circle is repeated that great social movement which has changed the world. If so simple a matter needed any other justification than the urgency of the missionary spirit, appeal could be made to the deepest principles of sociology.

Churches in depleted towns are of three kinds—the superfluous whose extinction is desirable, the vital and useful that can support themselves, and those whose preservation requires and justifies assistance. Churches of the first class require nothing of us except that we stay the waste of our sympathy and sternly foster the social wisdom that refuses to be burdened with an inheritance of religious institutions too ample for present needs. Churches of the second class must work out their own salvation, and it is an immediate and pressing duty to develop the consciousness of ability and fitness and opportunity, that needless shrinkage and depression may be checked, and that a great spiritual and social service may not suffer. Churches of the third class make a peculiar appeal, and this must be voiced here.

The plea of the home missionary churches should have the dignity and the force of the principles involved in it. There is first of all the claim of a church to live that it may fulfill its spiritual mission. What has been said in this chapter of the superfluity of churches is not intended to suggest any general withdrawal of the home missionary societies from their fields. Our wholesale criticism has its pertinence, but each case must be judged in view of all the local conditions. A missionary society must pursue a practical rather than an ideal policy. Until conditions beyond the control of any single body of men change, a responsible administration must be trusted. The presumption is that a church has a duty to live; the elimination of useless churches must be left to inexorable change, and the Christian conscience shrinks from church-killing with forethought. As a whole the home missionary churches amply vindicate their usefulness; no churches in city or country can show larger returns for the investment; a dollar, a Christian worker, a church member, means more for the kingdom in these churches than in any others. Year after year the home missionary churches report a success out of all proportion to their visible resources, and year after year they give men and women of priceless value to other communities. The familiar argument, moving on with irresistible statistics and with a convincing splendor of illustrious names, need not be rehearsed. Not every church on the dependent rolls, yet the typical home missionary church, has demonstrated its right to live.

The aided churches should make their appeal in the frank use of the federal principle without humiliation and without apology. When the people are too few to sustain a church, their inability is not their fault. And certainly when the reduction of numbers and wealth is due to changes in the very form of civilization, being a part of universal progress, those who suffer loss are justly entitled to aid from those who reap the benefit. There is one society, one national life, and all are members one of another. If the argument of this book has not failed, the plea of these enfeebled churches should be clear and emphatic and persuasive.

In the reconstruction of rural society—modified, revitalized, aided where there is need of help—the church will be an indestructible and dominating factor. Its social service is so fundamental that its consideration requires a chapter to itself.

CHAPTER XVII

THE CHURCH AS A SOCIAL CENTRE

THE social interpretation of the gospel involves no new departure. Even the Middle Ages succeeded in uniting the theology of Augustine and a passionate interest in the kingdom of God on earth; and the Puritan, in spite of an individualism as extreme as Bunyan portrayed, is remembered chiefly for his uncompromising interference with social usages and his brilliant quest of a theocracy. We take our place in the succession of those who have sought to make the world a fit habitation for the children of God when we seek to understand the social duty of the church. The country church must be more than a sect replenishing its ranks by propagandism; it must perpetuate the New England tradition of a church which is the spiritual aspect of a town.

In the early chapters of a " Modern Instance " Mr. Howells draws a mocking picture of the miscellaneous entertainments and diversions of a country church, representing the effort of a church to make itself a social centre as superseding a former spiritual interest. To turn even the most genial satire upon the attempt to embody the social passion of the time, betrays a singular unfamiliarity with current religious ideals. The church distinctly avows its social interest and does not hesitate to claim that this is an expression of a true religious fervor. The Christian religion is essentially social,—its great words being love and brotherhood and fellowship. Following after righteousness, the church must challenge and seek to reform that social order in which the moral life is expressed. Cherishing ideals of service and having an instinct of joy, the community of Christians is constrained to enrich as many lives as it can touch; and what is so available for this ministry as that spirit of friendliness in which all virtues thrive and gladness is set free?

The country town needs a social centre. The church need offer no apology for its ambition to take this place in the community, if an understanding of its mission brings this purpose into clear consciousness. Oftener there will be a cluster of social activities about the church with no distinct perception of their significance. And some churches, it must be confessed, are so slightly representative of the people that an assumption of this office on their part would be an impertinence. Sectarian divisions cause great confusion, and they are a most serious obstacle in the development of the most efficient social structure. Because they are so common and so baffling, it is a maxim in some circles that religion, like politics, must be ignored in fixing and developing a social centre. Education, being a universal interest, offers a more hopeful prospect, and there are many serious attempts to make the school the social centre of the town. Certainly much is to be said in behalf of the structure at whose centre is the group of kindred institutions—the school, the library, and the lecture hall.   These should unite the people, and from them should radiate influences to every part of the community.   The candidacy of the church for this office, however, is not so weak as the advocates of its rivals allege.   There are many favored towns which have but one church, and although such a church cannot command the interest of all the people, it is relieved from the chief embarrassments of religiously divided communities.   But these may be overestimated, for there is essential harmony of spirit among churches that occupy the same field, and the separation into social groups need not prevent a massing of the influences in which all share about a religious centre, which will be none the less real for having no visible location.   There is danger, also, of falling into error from over-simplification.   In fact the structure of a community is exceedingly complex ; it contains many social groups, each of which has its own centre.   All of these groups contribute in their several ways and degrees to the common life.   All that we need claim is that the church, or each of several churches, is a social centre to some good purpose. Ideally the one church should be the soul of the town and the centre of the social life ; practically each church must give a cordial welcome to competitors of many kinds.   And when we come to make careful discriminations, it will appear that the church is called to lay off upon other institutions important social functions as certainly as it is under obligation to assume its proper social leadership.

If now we ask what it means for the church to be a

social centre,—in the manner in which this is possible in all sorts of communities,—the country church, at least, must make some provision for social pleasure. It must do this because rural communities may have no diversions and entertainments if the church does not provide them. Usually, however, amusements will not be lacking, and then the duty of the church may be determined by the necessity of guarding its own people from coarse or sinful pleasures. The case can hardly be imagined in which a country church has not a distinct duty to plan for enjoyment; its children and young people should meet when religion is not even mentioned. It is found to be safest for them to meet frequently under the direction and care of the church. To send them into the world with no social training exposes them to grave perils, and to try to keep them out of the world with no social privileges is sheer folly. If young people demand social opportunity, older persons need social intercourse. All have a social nature to be cultivated, but the requirement of the young is imperative. "The church," says President Hyde rightly, "must provide directly or indirectly some modern equivalent for the huskings, apple bees, quiltings, and singing schools of the old days. In some way or other young men and young women must have opportunity for unconstrained intercourse, free from self-consciousness and artificiality. This may take the form of clubs, parties, picnics, excursions, or what you please. One rule is absolute: the church must not attempt to take away the theatre, the dance, the card party unless it can give in its

place, not merely a religious or intellectual substitute,
like a prayer-meeting or a literary society, but a
genuine social equivalent."

In providing for enjoyment the church uses one of
the great methods by which human society has developed. Association is never secure until it is pleasur-
able; in play the instinctive aversion of one person
for another is overcome, and the social mood is
fostered. Professor Giddings remarks that play is the
chief educational agency in animal communities and
that in the play-day of human childhood social sympathy, a social sense, and a social habit are evolved.
In his view rude sports and even harmful dissipations
make a large contribution to the social development
of barbarous races.[1] As individuals come together
with pleasure they change until finally they constitute
a society. It is plain, therefore, that the church which
aims at a perfected society must use in a refined and
more exalted way this essential factor in social evolution, and that the church which would be a social
centre must avail itself of the universal instinct for
play. There will be no attempt to furnish all the
wholesome enjoyment and festivity of the community.
It is enough if the church surrounds itself with a
joyousness of its own kind, filling some part of the
lamentable gap in rural pleasures by such entertain-
ment as should be easily possible for an association of
persons—the richest in joy and charm and kindness
that the town affords.

Fortunately happiness is not left behind in the

[1] The Principles of Sociology, pp. 116-121.

ascent of life. In the highest circles social opportunity is at its best. Fellowship in intelligence supersedes fellowship in sport. The church sociable is a somewhat daring experiment midway between the lower region of pure sport, where success is easy, and the higher sphere of intelligence, where the way is clear though few can walk in it. Without dancing or cards a company passes an evening in chief reliance upon conversation. From the evolutionary point of view dancing and cards are valuable because they enable people who cannot talk to spend a few hours together happily. Conversation—than which nothing is more uncertain or difficult—is the ultimate social pastime. It is not strange that movement on this social height is stiff and awkward, and that relief is sought in literary and musical and miscellaneous programmes. The best of these are simple lectures or addresses by invited guests, such as are not out of reach in ordinary villages. Thinking of the same theme for a half hour unites divided minds, and conversation before and afterwards has incentive and guidance. It must be said, however, that the church sociable is the chivalry of social effort, and that the brave and the fair have suffered much in its behalf.

In socializing men work serves as well as play. As people work together they acquire social skill and social adaptation; hence the church which sustains the greatest activity will lead in social progress. Here is the place to appraise those institutional methods which in addition to their worth for ministration are valuable, also, for their contribution to social facility.

In the country as in the city the justification of the methods known as institutional is, first, in the need of the community and, secondly, in their fitness to the local conditions. The church may undertake to fill whatever gaps there may be in the social organization. In the city a multitude of young people are not in homes; therefore the church in the midst of such a constituency wisely provides what substitute it can. Rooms are opened, interests are created, contacts are planned to keep young people out of the streets and the saloons and vile places of amusement, and to rescue them from the loneliness into which they shrink if they are too refined for coarse associations. In the country the family abides in its pristine strength, and the effort to take the young people out of their homes is needless and mischievous, except as their social nature requires indulgence and culture. Again in the city adults in large numbers lack the education that would fit them for the work to which their natural abilities are adequate. The evening school and classes for the study of technical subjects are highly serviceable; but in the country there is no such chasm between opportunity and training. In the city, also, the Roman Catholic church maintains the parochial school; in the country this is impossible, and if possible, it would be disastrously divisive. Education is provided by the country town, and the church has no duty here except in inspiration and suggestion and, perhaps, in offering to congenial groups the privilege of studying together some branch of the higher culture. The library should be a town institution; reading-rooms and lecture courses are best when they frankly ask the patronage and support of all the people; even clubs profit by independence. Although personal service has constant opportunity, the financial burden of the poor must rest solidly upon the town, for whose constant and adequate support the sporadic generosity of the church is no substitute. Nothing should be permitted to arrest the development of civic responsibility, nor to mar the pride of the people in the municipal hearth-stone, nor to discourage the social life clustering about it. The progress of civilization divides the social offices among many organs, and the church is reactionary that presumes to do what is well done by other institutions. The ideal social organization is complex,—the vital process employing many organs in the unity of a common life. The church should exercise a wise caution and resist the temptations of the monopolizing spirit, being willing to suffer effacement if thereby the community is served best. The family, the school, the town, societies, orders, social groups and institutions of many sorts—all have their place. A false ecclesiastical ambition would have the church absorb as many of these functions as possible, but it is far better that such development of institutionalism should be separate from the church, whose proper office is inspirational. The institutional expansion of the church is proper only when the social outfit is defective; then the church ought to fill the gaps.

Local conditions restrict institutional methods within comparatively narrow limits in the country. It is sheer

folly to attempt to repeat in the midst of farms those
social experiments that win great success in cities.[1]
Country people have long days of labor, and when at
last their work is done, they are tired. Plans for
spending evenings away from home must be few.
The gymnasium is excluded by the general weariness
at nightfall, although the public playground with a
simple gymnastic outfit is found to meet the countryman's love of sports in a wholesome way. The growing athletic interest has a valuable influence for social
unity, and gatherings of the people to witness con-
tests of schoolboys and young men would go far to
develop a town consciousness. Reading-rooms are
suited to the larger villages; but magazine and book
clubs are more practical and they should have indefinite multiplication. In the greater leisure of the future,
there will be opportunity for the Woman's Club, and
simple organizations of girls and boys for a variety of
purposes are commonly practicable. A literary
society will have its alternations of success and quiescence. Cooking classes with judicious instruction in
dietetics are sorely needed, but up to the present time

[1] "If these remarks mean anything, it is that we need new country
institutions developed from the country point of view, not merely city
and town institutions transplanted to the country" (L. H. Bailey,
"The Outlook to Nature," p. 130). This book came from the press
too late for the author's use, but it is a pleasure to find that it confirms
many views which he has attempted to present. Professor Bailey has
the exceptional merit of a naturalist who appreciates the larger as well
as the smaller aspects of nature; and these charming lectures, which
are the fruit of lifelong study of rural life, are enriched quite as much
from a rare poetic sympathy as from the scientific interest.

hunger has been too imperative to allow uncertain experiment on the part of the farmer's wife. There ought to be a development of University Extension pervading all rural towns, but the country must look to the colleges for the inauguration of this movement. Lecture courses under local management are eminently desirable. Village Improvement Societies are an imperative need, and their work is manifold.

It may be held with confidence that the country church has a considerable field for institutional service, after all restrictions are recognized. In the depleted community whose social outfit is imperilled and in the raw and backward town which has not possessed the full social equipment the church stands in the breach and should be ready to devise and sustain every useful ministry. In some cases the church itself will organize these activities within itself or under its care ; in other instances it will be content to stimulate independent organization for these ends. As towns grow and develop social institutions, the office of the church is more and more limited to the training of men and women for the social life, who without the initiative of the church bear the burden of the social welfare. In communities of the highest type the church will cease to be institutional, but the ordinary country church has no such prospect,—it must be all things to all men. Here then is a great field in which the adherents of the church may work together, and it will be found that as they pursue in common their task of promoting the general good, they will grow in like-mindedness, in social sympathy, and true social efficiency.

They will be bound together in work as well as play. Such a church has gone far towards making itself a social centre.

A familiar biological analogy suggests something far more important than these varied ministries of the church to the social life. In this view, the church is an organ having definite functions in the social body. In the division of labor the church becomes responsible for those services for which no other organ exists; these determine its imperative duty. Other services may be undertaken; these must not be neglected. These structural offices are a far more important social service of the church than anything yet considered. This unique function of the church came into view for a moment when it was suggested that in the ideal community the proper task of the church is the training of men and women for the duties of life, being inspirational rather than institutional. And if we ask how this formation of character goes forward, the answer is that it is incidental to public worship. The church is a social centre primarily and chiefly because it is the community organized for worship—the noblest of all the social functions.

In the future the social spirit must be the chief reliance in inducing the people to attend church, for it is no longer possible to prevent a wide desertion of the churches by the individualistic appeal. Indeed the break has already come, as the crowds at Sunday resorts attest. These deserters of the church, if they have not ceased to consider the grounds of their conduct, persuade themselves that they will receive more elsewhere than at church. The justice of this conclusion cannot be conceded, yet how is it possible to convince the irreligious of their mistake? Providentially the social appeal in behalf of religion is stronger than ever before, and there is reason to hope that as the social spirit develops, the abandonment of the churches will be arrested. Those who will not attend church for their own good may come to see that public worship is an indispensable function of social life. There is no more beautiful vision of human brotherhood than the assembly of the people of a community for fellowship in the highest things and for communion of spirit in the worship of God. The sectarian cleft has defeated the aspiration for unity in this most uplifting public exercise, so that the world still waits for this supreme social beatitude. Now that doctrinal antagonisms are eliminated, it should be possible to realize locally the aim of a national church. A single church in a town would be best of all, but unity of spirit may reach the essential ends where separate organizations cannot be immediately discarded. The one obstacle to this highest social unity is the preference of many of the people to have no share in public worship. As long as the attitude was concealed by an outward respect for the Sabbath, its social significance passed unnoticed; but the recent organization of Sunday desecration with costly mechanism and elaborate outfit and immense assemblies has brought to light the deep social division. There are now two camps with numbers and equipments nearly equal. It is a most serious question whether society can stand the strain, and when the peril is fully appreciated, the value of public worship will receive a new estimate in all thoughtful minds.

That there may be a common life, the people must have the same thoughts; they must recognize the same standard of morals; they must cherish the same great ends. Public opinion, the social conscience, the common ideal, are as important in the town as nerves in the body. Apart from the churches there is no adequate provision for these necessary elements of the social life. Certainly no other agency rivals the church in directing the minds of the people towards great themes. The essential thing is that truth and moral law and spiritual worth and beauty should be pressed upon attention until extensive spheres of their regnant influence develop; this can be done by public discussions such as those of the pulpit. There is no substitute for this unifying power. The school molds the child, but its influence ceases when most needed. The press speaks with many voices, chronicling results rather than presenting formative principles. And besides, it is urban or national, and is adapted to counteract provincialism rather than build up local sentiment. Literature is incompetent for this office, for the book has comparatively few readers and does little more than influence those who lead the masses. The personal advocacy by the human voice in an assembly of the people is the natural means of disseminating ideas, and there is no such intelligent, earnest, and continuous force, unifying public opinion and forming the social conscience, as the preaching of Christian truths and duties to a worshipping congregation in the midst of the powerful impressions of the house of God.

This function of the church must not be conceived too abstractly. Every man who desires to be honest should be able to depend upon his neighbor's understanding of the requirement of honesty. The pulpit should be strong and clear enough in its utterance to provide a basis for all ordinary transactions. It should be able to define the fundamental political obligations, so that every good citizen may feel that every other good citizen cherishes the common standard of civic duty. It should enforce neighborly obligation with such vigor as to make the observance of the Golden Rule an established reciprocity, bringing to an end needless sacrifice on the part of him who faithfully loves his brother. Exalted to its rightful place, the pulpit provides the moral basis for all social intercourse and coöperation.

The country preacher has a special privilege of interpreting the wider movements of the age. The tendency of rural life is to beget a shrinking from the progress of the world and to develop a jealous and pessimistic temper. Not the least of its services to the social life is the contribution of the country pulpit to the hospitable and expectant view of modern progress. The success of the young people when they go out into the greater world is due in no small degree to the sympathetic and inspiriting interpretation of the age by the preacher in the village church. To inspire in the hearts of young men and young women confidence that modern industry and progress rest upon

honesty and fidelity and ministry and sympathy, and
to drive from the mind the lie that success is won by
smartness and craft and selfishness, is well nigh the
greatest of all contributions to society.

For such teachings as these the country offers a
favorable field. In the rural town there is a certain
ripeness for the kingdom of heaven—the final social
achievement. Organization is but elementary; a new
social order may come with the least opposition and
at the lowest cost. Economic and social equality are
not such tantalizing dreams as in the city. The richer
and more highly educated are elevated but slightly
above their neighbors, and they cannot leave behind
them the common scale and style of living. In
hastening the coming of the kingdom within its narrow borders, the country church renders a great social
service to the world at large, for the simple type of
the better social order embodies the essential principle,
—the microcosm reveals the order and beauty of the
larger world.

Great as is the ministry of moral and social instruction, it is but the beginning of the benefit of public
worship in the community. The unification of society
requires that softening of asperities, that quickening
of sympathy, that elevation of ideals, that regeneration
of the moral life which are linked to religion as the
one adequate dynamic. It is impossible to tell
whether the prophetic or the priestly office of the
church contributes more to the rise of that sense of
brotherhood under the divine Fatherhood which is the
fountain of all social forces. The church does not

merely teach a doctrine of truth or duty; it has a peculiar power of setting man forward in the better life. This taking of man the sinner and setting him in the very presence of God, forgiven and dedicated to the highest ideals, is the essence of the church's priestly office. The drawing near to God in penitence and confession and aspiration and consecration is the element in worship that gives it saving power. The teaching of religion from the pulpit is essential for the development of unity in the higher sentiments and ideals and the teaching of ethics is indispensable in the formation of public opinion and the social conscience; equally necessary is the movement of divine power upon the hearts of the people that they may do the things they understand. The common confession before God is the sovereign cure for egoism and the beginning of humility and love. This is "that sublime ascent of soul, that common flight of love, in which all individuality is lost, all personal regards absorbed, and the vision of heaven and God melts the many minds and many voices of the church in one."[1] As social unity develops, it will find expression more and more in the priestly offices of the church; and these in turn will be the great incentive of the social spirit. Preaching will not be less important, but it will be conceived as a part of a larger whole—as a single element in worship.

It is not the minister who is primarily prophet or priest in the Christian church. The preacher speaks for the people. The sermon is the confession of faith for

[1] James Martineau, " Endeavors After the Christian Life," p. 123.

the congregation, declaring what each man would speak as his thought takes shape in the presence of God. There is a fine attuning of minds in consequence of which the words spoken awaken responsive chords. Truth and exhortation are freighted with the feeling and conviction of the assembly. So true is this that a spiritual congregation preaches a spiritual sermon, and a worldly congregation preaches a worldly sermon. The minister may purpose otherwise, but a force he cannot resist shapes his speech. Congregations are organic things; they differ like living creatures. That which creeps cannot run, and that which runs cannot fly. A creeping congregation may resolve to run by calling an active minister, or to fly by securing a soaring one; but the end is that strength is palsied and wings cannot lift. The preacher, it is true, declares a divine message; he heralds a gospel in a world of sin; he is to rebuke, convict, persuade; he must carry on a controversy with his hearers, who gather for warning and correction. If he must not abjectly reflect the spirit of the congregation, lest preaching lose its authority, its vitality, and its urgency, neither can he isolate himself lest he become incapable of fostering fraternity and degenerate into a common scold. The ideal is that the minister should speak with a peculiar authority because he represents a congregation whose experience matches revelation and gospel. He is the voice for many witnesses.

If the whole church preaches through the minister as prophet, much more does it worship through the minister as priest. In prayer the minister speaks for the people; through him the people make confession and offer thanksgiving and praise ; through him also they utter their petitions and intercessions. The gospel of reconciliation is committed to the whole church—the common priesthood of believers. The keys of the kingdom of heaven are given unto all those who have been added to the first confessor that Jesus is the Christ, the Son of the living God.

Minister and people may sometimes lose that unity in which is social power, and just here is the peculiar difficulty of our time. In the realm of truth the minister has advanced more rapidly than the people, so that often the congregation fails to hear from the pulpit the familiar formulas of faith expressed in the terms grown dear in tradition. In the realm of life, on the other hand, the people have felt strange influences of new times ; in their bewilderment they have turned to the preacher with importunate appeal for guidance, which they have not always found. Wherever the pulpit has parted from the living faith of the people, or the people have ceased to illustrate the ideals of life for which the pulpit pleads, there is loss of influence in the community. At the earliest moment the congregation should offer the response of conviction to the new statements of truth, and as quickly as possible the preacher should learn how to present the ideals which command the loyalty of. our worshipping assemblies.

The witnessing congregation, through the testimony of preaching and through the changed lives that are the final result of worship, speaks to the entire community. Organizations of many kinds exert an influence far beyond the circle of their members and adherents; this is preëminently true of the Christian church, whose power for good far exceeds the visible operation of its forces. Long before the whole body of the people can be brought to profess its faith or to participate in its worship, the community is pervaded by its teachings and inspired by its ideals. It is now possible to find a scientific explanation of this fact.

Modern psychology makes much of suggestion. A single person may have hypnotic power over a crowd; a crowd may have intimidating power over the individual. A homogeneous body acting upon a heterogeneous mass has both hypnotic and intimidating power. So impressible is the mind and so prone to imitation that few persons can resist this mental inoculation until they become immune by frequent repetition of the process. Here is the secret of the pervasive power of preaching; the man who has the power to utter a fresh message in the ears of a congregation with such vividness and passion as to send awakened men and women out into the community to talk of what they have heard, does far more than appeal to those who fill the pews. The voice sounding from the pulpit reverberates from side to side of the parish, and all the people, whether attending church or not, feel the shock of the intellectual storm. This is not always a sound of voices, for the silent influences of purified and ennobled character come under the same law. By word and deed and life the church diffuses the preacher's utterance; although the medium often is dull and without resonance, it has its great place in the divine method and in the aggregate multiplies preaching many fold.

For such forces as these the country affords peculiar opportunity. The immensity of the city overwhelms the preacher and the church. Only a Beecher or a Phillips Brooks is an adequate spiritual battery for a great city; but an ordinary man, preaching to a small congregation, need not despair of influencing a rural town. Social psychology will yet vindicate the old-fashioned revival, which was a general attention to religion developing in a perfectly simple and natural way. Whenever the church can so coördinate and reiterate its testimony as to overcome the unstable equilibrium of the surrounding mass of suggestible minds, a revival of religion is sure to come. If any refuse to deduce so conservative a conclusion from such modern premises, they need not hesitate to recognize the method of successful agitation. Reform is a social phenomenon, social in its progress as well as in its result. The worship of the church sends into the community many ramifying but accordant influences of high potency.

The church is capable of this incomparable service in the social process because it is the steward of the spiritual treasure of humanity. Coming from a higher sphere, or dwelling among men in open vision of a better order in which the authority of God and the supremacy of the spirit and the obligations of love are self-evident verities, Jesus is the unique regenerator of society. In worship the church participates in the heavenly vision. From heaven the New Jerusalem descends. To substitute for this spiritual intuition of the worshipper a mere scientific sociology, to teach even social Christianity apart from its inspiration in communion with God, to urge the Golden Rule without the tidal uplift of the coming kingdom, excites the retort that such principles are impracticable in the present world. The distinction of Christianity is its power to kindle a passion for its ideals which sends men into the strife of the time to know no rest until they behold the earthly counterpart of the divine beauty.

The church is the community worshipping, and when the worship of the people is efficiently and fittingly maintained, an essential social function is discharged, and one organ of society does its proper work. The view of the church as a social centre discovers many forms of fellowship and service, but all others compared with worship are no more than the twinkling of a star at whose heart is a steady splendor. It is time to correct the emphasis which has been misplaced so long in popular discussion and to give to worship its just recognition as the supreme function of the church. The church must not part with its birthright in perennial privilege and power for the savory pottage that satisfies the hunger of an hour. In rustic simplicity and the wild mood of nature Esau forfeited his inheritance, which passed to the far-seeing Jacob. The country church must beware of the mistake of the impulsive hunter, for pottage, though for a multitude, is not the solution of the human problem. In the solitude of the Judean hills Jesus met the same temptation to concentrate attention upon lower needs, but that greatest social founder refused to change stones into bread. Beset by the old temptation, the church must learn to live by every word from the mouth of God.

Nowhere is the country church ideal, but under the constraint of need it has found out in some degree the way of actual service to living men. In some measure it succeeds in imparting courage, inspiring kindness, developing brotherhood, creating character, helping men live under the eternal order. The community needs nothing so much as a church to interpret life, to diffuse common standards of morals, to plead for the public interest, to inculcate unselfishness, neighborliness, coöperation, to uphold ideals, to stand for the supremacy of the spirit. And in the depleted town, with shattered institutions and broken hopes, in the perplexity of changing times, in peril of degeneracy, the church is the vital centre which must be saved at any cost. In the readjustments of the times the country church has suffered, but if in its sacrifices it has learned to serve the community, it lives and will live. On the fidelity and intelligence, on the consecration and fervor of churches called to this high function in social dynamics, depends the issue whether there shall be a country of peasants and serfs incapable of civic coöperation, or of freemen and citizens of public spirit; whether there shall be a human wilderness environing imperilled cities, or a paradise of homes over all the hills out of which shall flow rivers of life for urban redemption. " It is certain the country people would soon degenerate into a kind of savages and barbarians, were there not such frequent returns of a stated time, in which the whole village meet together with their best faces, and in their cleanliest habits, to converse with one another upon indifferent subjects, hear their duties explained to them, and join together in adoration of the Supreme Being." [1]   That many things dishearten is true, but why magnify them?   Only as we maintain an open vision for the ideal can we hope

> "To preserve as things above all price
> The old domestic morals of the land,
> Her simple manners and the stable worth
> That dignified and cheered a low estate,
> . . .   the character of peace,
> Sobriety and order, and chaste love,
> And honest dealing, and untainted speech,
> And pure good-will, and hospitable cheer;
> That made the very thought of country life
> A thought of refuge, for a mind detained
> Reluctantly amid the bustling crowd." [2]

[1] *The Spectator*, No. 112.
[2] Wordsworth, " The Excursion," Book Eighth.

THE LAST WORD

Our study of the country town is at an end. We have endeavored to face candidly the havoc of the times, giving patience and labor as required to trace through recent history that vast industrial revolution which has thinned the rural population and altered every condition of country life. We have welcomed cheering growth to meet new demands, and have followed with increasing courage the main trend of hope. We have sought to know the worst that the evolutionist can tell of the loss of the best of the people decade after decade, and have hailed with gratitude the compensations of a new and powerful environment. We have discerned the mighty uplift of the nation— that partnership of all communities in which the feeblest are represented and in whose strength they live. We have seen towns maintain their vitality, draw their depleted forces into stronger unity, and emerge from the trial as indestructible fountain-heads of democracy. We have marvelled at the country church—the bush burning with the presence of God and abiding unconsumed—the centre and soul of the community. We began with the study of food and clothing; we lingered long over personal characteristics; we ascended at last to the vision of a spiritual kingdom. And what shall abide in memory? The argument has failed if the map is stained with the dull pigments that tell the story of

depletion and decay so deeply that the living green of
life adjusted to the new times does not define a broad
belt of hope across the land.

For those of stout heart there are visions of the
country town akin to such as have kindled the imagination,—of a community beautiful with the ideal elements of Plato's Republic and possessing the substantial qualities of Aristotle's democracies, without the
freakishness of the one and the high explosiveness of
the other. This country town of our hopes is no
Utopia in far seas, no inaccessible City in the Sun, but
a human development actually taking shape before our
eyes,—a divine society wrought out of the vicissitudes
of men in the painful process of evolution. Though
the eye that watches grows weary and the heart that
hopes for it faints, yet the swift years will bring that
social triumph; and when at last men look upon its
full beauty and joy, multitudes will be found dwelling
near to nature,—ultimate felicity retaining the primal
gladness of a country life. Other multitudes may
dwell in cities, but in that far adjustment differences
of country and city will be but lights and shades in
the common happiness. Meanwhile though the pat-
tern is of God, the labor is of men. The movement is
on the cosmic scale and beyond the power of any man
to thwart; and yet that vast progress gathers into itself
the contributions that men make, and its momentum
is the aggregate of what men do. In every community the issue depends upon generous deeds, tireless
diligence, and steadfast patience.

INDEX

ABANDONED farms, inevitable, 26–28, 146; no longer significant, 53; general account of, 66-69

Adams, Henry, on former religious conditions, 260

Agricultural exports, amount of, 46

Agricultural machinery, invention of, 21; efficiency of, 21; diminishes rural population, 23–28

Alger, Edith G., 189

Amaron, C. E., on foreign stock in New England, 159

Anderson, Mary P., 4; on nature study, 187, 188

Aristotle, on size of a city, 78; on equality, 150; on society, 224; on democracy, 227

Arnold, Matthew, on equality, 150; on individualism, 224; on the state, 254

BAILEY, L. H., on country institutions, 286

Baldwin, James Mark, on organic selection, 174, 175

Beef, price of, 49–51; production leaving the ranch, 50, 78

Bell, C. H., 20

Berkshire County Eagle, on consolidation of farms, 72

Boston Herald, on consolidation of farms, 72; on rural degeneracy, 102

Boyle, J. E., on extinction of churches, 266

Brewer, W. H., on education of the farm, 24; on abandoned farms, 28

Brierly, J., 94

Bryce, James, on rural administration, 243

Bushnell, Horace, on age of homespun, 12, 127; on our ancestors, 134; on danger of barbarism, 134, 179

CAPITAL, organized, 230; owned in the country, 238, 239

Church, the country, local decadence, 99–101; former state of, 258–260; in growing towns, 261–263; consolidation, 264–267; characteristics, 267–272; in depleted towns, 273–275; aid necessary, 276, 277; a social centre, 278–300

Cities, growth of, 28–35, 54, 55; rural partnership with, 35–45, 97, 211, 232; market for farms, 46–53; small cities thriving, 86–89; attraction of, 54, 194–196; separation of classes in, 205; political power of, 228, 233; the church in, 257

Comstock, J. M., on new churches, 266

Corn, price of, 47–49; in New England, 83

Country life, attractive, 182; dull, 195; social intercourse, 201–205; farmsteads, 244, 246

Country, the, progress in, 28; base for city, 29, 35–45, 210,

230; zone of growth, 77–91,
111, 115–117; local decadence,
95–106, 110, 116; bad heritage
in, 123–135; political power
of, 229–233, 239; wealth in,
238, 239; prospects of, 301.
See Rural Character, Rural
Population
County, the, in the political system, 249–251
Cowper, on love of the country,
182
Coxe, Tench, on household manufactures, 13; on textile machines, 19; on exports, 46
Crime, in the country, 101, 113,
114
Crothers, S. M., on theorizing,
107

DANTE, 183
Darwin, on natural selection, 172
Davis, R. M., on fixed charge of
the family, 69
Degeneracy, rural, local only, 95–
106, 110, 116; from superior
ancestry, 124; distinguished
from unfitness, 135
Depletion, rural, extent of, 57–
76; in Illinois, 61; in New
Hampshire, 62–64; duration
of, 64; standard of, 65; abandoned farms, 66–69; consolidation of farms, 69–75; moral
effects of, 95–117; selection by,
122, 123; social consequences
of, 221, 247, 263–267, 299
De Vries, mutation theory of, 172,
199
Dinsmore, Charles A., 4
Divorce, in the country, 110
Dorchester, Daniel, on religious
progress, 263
Dwight, Timothy, on size of
towns, 248

EDUCATION, of the farm, 24; agricultural, 217; town system
of, 252, 284; state aid of, 254.
See Schools, Nature Study
Eggleston, N. H., on country
life, 194
Embargo of 1807, effect of, 14
Emerson, R. W., on increase of
population, 38; on reinforcement of cities, 97; on to-day,
127; on our ancestors, 129; on
manners, 144; originality of,
200
Emmons, Nathanael, on former
moral conditions, 128
Environment, power of, 175–180;
personal, 196, 201; new factors in, 209–221, 225
Equality, promoted by depletion,
147–150
Evolution, by natural selection,
121–123, 171; mutation theory
of, 172; by germinal selection,
173; by organic selection, 174–
177

FAIRCHILD, G. T., on prices of
farm products, 47
Family, fixed charge of the, 69,
70
Farms, price of, 53; consolidation of, 69–75; intensive cultivation, 81–85
Federal power, held in check,
242, 251
Federal principle, the, 226–229,
241
Federal regulation of industries,
52, 230–240; social consequences of, 235–240
Fiske, John, on progress, 10; on
rural Virginia, 31; on settlement of New England, 131;
on environment, 170; on the
federal principle, 226
Foreign stock, pressure of, 151–
166; assimilation of, 167, 205
Fowler, Frederick H., 4, 68

Metropolitan America

AN ARNO PRESS COLLECTION

Adams, Thomas. **The Design of Residential Areas:** Basic Considerations, Principles, and Methods. (Harvard City Planning Studies, Vol. VI). 1934.

Anderson, Wilbert L. **The Country Town:** A Study of Rural Evolution. 1906.

Arnold, Bion J. **Report on the Improvement and Development of the Transportation Facilities of San Francisco.** Submitted to the Mayor and the Board of Supervisors, City of San Francisco. March, 1913. 1913.

Association for the Improvement of the Condition of the Poor. **Housing Conditions in Baltimore.** Report of a Special Committee of the Association for the Improvement of the Condition of the Poor and the Charity Organization Society. Submitting the Results of an Investigation Made by Janet E. Kemp. 1907.

Bassett, Edward M. **Zoning:** The Laws, Administration, and Court Decisions During the First Twenty Years. 1936.

Bauer, Catherine. **Modern Housing.** 1934.

Case, Walter H. **History of Long Beach and Vicinity.** (Volume 1). 1927.

Chamberlin, Everett. **Chicago and Its Suburbs.** 1874.

Chapin, E[dwin] H[ubbell]. **Humanity in the City.** 1854.

Coit, Stanton. **Neighborhood Guilds:** An Instrument of Social Reform. 1891.

Comey, Arthur C[oleman]. **Transition Zoning.** (Harvard City Planning Studies, Vol. V). 1933.

Covington, Kentucky, City Planning and Zoning Commission. **Comprehensive Plan for Covington, Kentucky, and Environs.** [1932].

Goodnow, Frank J. **City Government in the United States.** 1910.

Hinman, Albert Greene. **Population Growth and Its Demands Upon Land for Housing in Evanston, Illinois.** 1931.

Hubbard, Theodora Kimball and Henry Vincent Hubbard. **Our Cities To-Day and To-Morrow:** A Survey of Planning and Zoning Progress in the United States. 1929.

Kellogg, Paul Underwood, editor. **The Pittsburgh District Civic Frontage** (Pittsburgh Survey, Vol. 5). 1914.

Kellogg, Paul Underwood, editor. **Wage-Earning Pittsburgh** (Pittsburgh Survey, Vol. 6). 1914.

Knowles, Morris. **Industrial Housing:** With Discussion of Accompanying Activities; Such as Town Planning, Street Systems, Development of Utility Services, and Related Engineering and Construction Features. 1920.

Lindsey, Ben B. and Rube Borough. **The Dangerous Life.** 1931.

Marsh, Benjamin Clarke. **An Introduction to City Planning:** Democracy's Challenge to the American City. With a Chapter on the Technical Phases of City Planning by George B. Ford. [1909].

Maxwell, Sidney D. **The Suburbs of Cincinnati:** Sketches, Historical and Descriptive. 1870.

Metropolitan Police Manuals—1871, 1913. Introduction by Richard C. Wade. 1974.

Moehlman, Arthur B. **Public Education in Detroit.** 1925.

National Municipal League. Committee on Metropolitan Government. **The Government of Metropolitan Areas in the United States.** Prepared by Paul Studenski with the Assistance of the Committee on Metropolitan Government. 1930.

National Resources Committee. **Our Cities:** Their Role in the National Economy. Report of the Urbanism Committee to the National Resources Committee. 1937.

New York City. Board of Aldermen. Committee on General Welfare. **Preliminary Report of the Committee on General Welfare in the Matter of a Request of the Conference of Organized Labor Relative to Educational Facilities.** Meeting of June 26, 1917. 1917.

New York City. Staten Island Improvement Commission. **Report of a Preliminary Scheme of Improvements.** 1871.

Ogburn, William F. **Social Characteristics of Cities:** A Basis for New Interpretations of the Role of the City in American Life. 1937.

Pink, Louis H. **The New Day in Housing.** 1928.

Powell, Hickman. **Ninety Times Guilty.** 1939.

Regional Plan Association. **From Plan to Reality.** 1933/1938/1942. 3 volumes in one.

Regional Plan of New York and Its Environs. 2 volumes. 1929/1931.

Regional Survey of New York and Its Environs. 10 volumes. 1927-1931.

Simonds, Thomas C. **History of South Boston;** Formerly Dorchester Neck, Now Ward XII of the City of Boston. 1857.

Smythe, William E. **City Homes on Country Lanes:** Philosophy and Practice of the Home-in-a-Garden. 1921.

Straus, Nathan. **The Seven Myths of Housing.** 1944.

Studies of Suburbanization in Connecticut. Numbers 1-3. 1936/1938/1939.

Toulmin, Harry Aubrey, Jr. **The City Manager:** A New Profession. 1916.

U.S. Public Health Service. **Municipal Health Department Practice for the Year 1923.** Based Upon Surveys of the 100 Largest Cities in the United States Made by the United States Public Health Service in Cooperation with the Committee on Administrative Practice, American Public Health Association. Public Health Bulletin No. 164. 1926.

U.S. Senate. Committee on the District of Columbia. **City Planning.** Hearing Before the Committee on the District of Columbia, United States Senate, on the Subject of City Planning. 61st Congress, 2nd Session, Senate Document No. 422. 1910.

U.S. Senate. Juvenile Court of the District of Columbia. **Message from the President of the United States Transmitting a Letter from the Judge of the Juvenile Court of the District of Columbia Submitting a Report Covering the Work of the Juvenile Court During the Period From July 1, 1906, to June 30, 1926.** 69th Congress, 2nd Session, Senate Document No. 236. 1927.

Upson, Lent D. **Practice of Municipal Administration.** 1926.

West Side Studies. Carried on Under the Direction of Pauline Goldmark. 1914. 2 volumes in one.

Wilcox, Delos F[ranklin]. **Great Cities in America:** Their Problems and Their Government. 1910.

Zueblin, Charles. **American Municipal Progress.** 1916.

DATE DUE

OCT 22 '88			
DEC 1 '88			
SEP 4 199/			
GAYLORD			PRINTED IN U.S.A